Quarto is the authority on a wide range of topics.
Quarto educates, entertains and enriches the lives of
our readers—enthusiasts and lovers of hands-on living.
www.QuartoKnows.com

© 2017 Quarto Publishing Group USA Inc.
Text © 2017 Garret Romaine
Photography © 2017 Quarto Publishing Group USA Inc.

First Published in 2017 by Quarry Books, an imprint of The Quarto Group,
100 Cummings Center, Suite 265-D, Beverly, MA 01915, USA.
T (978) 282-9590 F (978) 283-2742 QuartoKnows.com

Quarry Books titles are also available at discount for retail, wholesale, pro-
motional, and bulk purchase. For details, contact the Special Sales Manager
by email at specialsales@quarto.com or by mail at The Quarto Group, Attn:
Special Sales Manager, 401 Second Avenue North, Suite 310, Minneapolis,
MN 55401, USA.

10 9 8 7 6 5 4 3 2 1

ISBN: 978-1-63159-285-0

Digital edition published in 2017
eISBN: 978-1-63159-405-2

Library of Congress Cataloging-in-Publication Data

Romaine, Garret.
Geology lab for kids.
ISBN 9781631592850 (flexi-bind)
1. Geology--Experiments--Juvenile literature. 2. Science
   projects--Juvenile literature.
QE29 .R738 2017
550.78--dc23

2017005836

Cover and Book Design: Kathie Alexander
Cover Images: Front cover images by Shutterstock, except bottom left
by Patrick Smith Photography. Back cover images by Patrick Smith
Photography, except top and bottom by Shutterstock.
Photography: Patrick Smith Photography, except images by Shutterstock
on pages 6, 9, 12, 20, 30, 42, 52, 54, 64, 72, 82, 86, 96, 104, 106 (top),
109 (left), 110, 118, 124 (top), 126, 132, and 134 (top); Garret Romaine: pages
92, 114 (left), and 128 (top).

Printed in China

Borax, also known by its chemical name sodium tetraborate, is a
trademarked product in the United States from the Rio Tinto Group.
In this book, Borax is used as a material in labs 4 and 7.

GEOLOGY
LAB FOR KIDS

52 PROJECTS TO EXPLORE ROCKS, GEMS, GEODES, CRYSTALS, FOSSILS, AND OTHER WONDERS OF THE EARTH'S SURFACE

QUARRY

GARRET ROMAINE

CONTENTS

INTRODUCTION

Geology is the science of the Earth and learning to describe what you see so that someone else can understand. Once you get good at talking about the world around you, it's not hard to take that to the next level and figure out what happened to the Earth in the past, even if you can't see it happening today. Nobody has ever traveled to the middle of the Earth, but by making models based on places we have been, we think we know what's going on there. That's science—make a prediction, see if you can prove it, and then apply it to bigger questions.

In this book, you will learn a lot about the way things happen and why. You'll be introduced to the science behind processes you see all around you, and you'll learn to think about the Earth in new and exciting ways. Some of the most important parts of geology come down to very simple concepts—gravity, friction, heat, and water. Some things you'll learn about are:

How to make your own crystals. Learn how crystals form and how to tell them apart. All rocks contain crystals, so this is a perfect place to begin.

The differences between major rock types. Learn how the three main groups of rocks form. You'll discover the forces behind igneous, sedimentary, and metamorphic rocks.

Identification and prospecting. See how scientists tell gems from ordinary crystals and how they learn to look for valuable rocks. Once you learn how to tell one mineral from another, you can start to identify the rocks you find all around you.

How things break down (entropy). See how Earth's forces take fresh, young lava flows and turn them into sand at the beach. The sun plays a part, too, and so do plants. Entropy is the idea that everything breaks down eventually. Steel will rust, and mountains will crumble.

Fossils are the clues of life. Our planet has an amazing fossil record to discover. Learn how scientists uncover clues about what Earth was like millions of years ago.

Why space rocks are important. Learn how comets and meteorites can rearrange the Earth's surface.

Rocks can be more than just rocks. Now that you know what's going on inside a rock or crystal, you'll see what you can do with rocks and minerals in work and play. There are lots of ways to display your treasures and use them to create art or everyday objects. Early humans used the materials around them for tools and you can, too.

Geology uses a set of vocabulary. Many of the words are ancient, dating back to the earliest times. Many foreign languages have found their way into geology as well. For example, the German words *schist* (pronounced "shist") and *gneiss* (pronounced "nice") both describe certain metamorphic rocks. Two Hawaiian words—*aa* (pronounced "ah-ah") and *pahoehoe* (pronounced "pa-hoy-hoy")— are used to describe lava flows, as there is so much volcanic activity on the Hawaiian islands. Aa lava is jagged and blocky, while pahoehoe lava is ropy and runny. These are just some of many examples.

Geology is based on observations and predictions that are part of the scientific model. Fortunately, the Earth works in a way we can understand, so if we can make the right model, we can use what we see in that model to predict other forces. We can measure things at a small scale, and we can make models to teach others. Even simple, fun projects can show the larger world at work. The labs and projects in this book will help you understand how much fun it is to learn about the world around you.

The best part is that most of these labs don't require a lot of expensive materials; many of them are easy to complete with items you find in your parents' kitchen or garage. But if you want to get super serious about understanding the world around you, this book will help you with that, too. Some of the materials will take a little more searching to find, and you may want to get help ordering items online that you can't easily track down. That can be part of the fun, too—you may get to go to thrift stores or second-hand stores to find used pots and pans, for example. You should also expect to visit a craft store to find some of the items you'll need.

And finally, be sure to visit a local rock and gem shop to find samples, books, tools, and advice on how to begin your own collection.

Over the years, I have spent countless hours working with kids just like you in lectures, at demonstrations, and even as a merit badge counselor, helping them understand the world around them. Many of the labs here are time-tested, having been around for years. But some are completely new or bring a new twist to an old idea. We'll start with simple concepts and then connect the dots to bigger ideas. In that way, these labs are like building blocks: start small and keep building. At some point, you'll probably find that you are learning how more and more pieces of the puzzle fit together. That's always been the most enjoyable for me, showing others how all the different things they already know can apply. It's always a lot of fun to go to the beach and pick up a few rocks, but when you know how to identify the rocks and explain how they got there, you feel like a detective solving a big riddle. Some of you may even go on to careers in the Earth sciences or become planetary scientists who travel to distant locales. I hope that's the case!

Let's get started. And remember: No one likes a messy lab partner!

IDENTIFYING ROCKS AND MINERALS

Rocks and minerals are the building blocks of the Earth. Minerals have a chemical formula, with an exact number of atoms of different elements. For example, calcite is $CaCO_3$—it has one calcium atom, one carbon atom, and three oxygen atoms. Minerals can be identified with tests for streak, hardness, crystal angle, and density, which you will learn in these labs. Rocks are made up of different minerals, in lots of combinations, and they can be glued, pressed, or melted together in many ways. To identify rocks, you need to know what minerals are in them, how they are held together, and how they formed. You will also learn about the three "families" of rocks: sedimentary, igneous, and metamorphic.

Shown here are many of the most common minerals that you can find, plus a few that are rare and valuable. Most of the rocks listed here are very common. If you can learn to identify them, you can start to explain the world around you.

Minerals

Calcite

Epidote

Feldspar

Fluorite

Garnet

Gold

Gypsum

Jade

Malachite

Muscovite mica

Pyrite

Quartz

Rocks

Agate

Basalt

Chalcedony

Chert

Conglomerate

Gneiss

Granite

Jasper

Limestone

Marble

Meteorite

Mudstone

Obsidian

Opal

Petrified wood

Quartzite

Rhyolite

Sandstone

Schist

UNIT
1

SINGULAR CRYSTALS

Maybe you've heard this joke: "How do you eat an elephant?" The answer is "one bite at a time." So, how do you "build" the Earth? That's simple, too: one crystal at a time.

Crystals come in a variety of shapes that scientists call *habits*. Common crystal habits include squares, triangles, and six-sided hexagons. Usually, crystals form when liquids cool, such as when you create ice cubes. Many times, crystals form in ways that do not allow for perfect shapes. If conditions are too cold, too hot, or there isn't enough source material, they can form strange, twisted shapes.

But when conditions are right, we see beautiful displays. Usually, this involves a slow, steady environment where the individual atoms have plenty of time to join and fit perfectly into what's known as the *crystal lattice*. This is the basic structure of atoms that is seen time after time. Crystals build in size when more and more atoms can find a place in the lattice to attach themselves.

In these labs, we'll create a liquid that allows the atoms plenty of time to join together. Sometimes, this involves starting with a "seed" crystal. The seed is already formed correctly and gives the atoms a chance to attach the right way. Sometimes crystals just want to form as a sheet, but that's not pretty. We want to see the beauty of nature, so we're going to use a seed to form the crystals that we want.

TASTY TREATS

Build a solid sugar crystal, sometimes called rock candy.

MATERIALS

- **1 cup (236 ml) of water**
- **Pan for boiling water**
- **3+ cups (600+ g) of white sugar**
- **Metal stirring spoon**
- **3–4 drops of food coloring of any color**
- **12″ (30 cm) of rough yarn or twine**
- **Scissors**
- **6″ (15 cm) pencil**
- **½-quart (473 ml) narrow-mouth glass Mason jar**
- **Round, hard ring-shaped candy (or other clean weight)**
- **Paper towel, napkin, or washcloth**

 Safety Tips

- Be cautious around the stove to avoid burns.
- Ask an adult for help boiling the water.

PROTOCOL

STEP 1: Add the water to the pan and boil the water on the stove. A microwave is not recommended.

STEP 2: Stir in the sugar slowly, adding as much as possible until it starts to build up at the bottom. Don't stop: you want your solution to be saturated.

STEP 3: Add a few drops of food coloring to make a rich color. Let cool.

STEP 4: Cut a piece of yarn or twine that is 1 inch (2.5 cm) longer than the height of your jar.

STEP 5: Tie one end of the twine or yarn around the pencil, leaving enough string to dangle the length of your jar without touching the bottom. Tie the other end around the piece of candy.

STEP 6: Moisten the string thoroughly with water, and then sprinkle lightly with sugar so that you create small "seed" crystals. Let dry for ten minutes.

STEP 10: Check on the string after a day; it should already host small, square sugar crystals.

STEP 11: Leave the string in the solution for at least a week. You can add more solution if you want to grow bigger crystals.

Creative Enrichment

1. What happens if you use fishing line or very smooth string?

2. Use a magnifying glass or hand lens to look at the hardened crystals. What shape are they? Would you call that a square or a cube?

3. What would happen if there were twice as much water—would the sugar ever crystallize on the string?

STEP 7: Pour the cooled water mixture into the jar. The solution needs to be cooled so that it won't dissolve your seed crystal. Avoid pouring any of the little sugar crystals from the bottom of the pan.

STEP 8: Place the pencil across the mouth of the jar so the candy floats in the mixture.

STEP 9: Place a paper towel, napkin, or washcloth over the jar and set it aside in a corner of the kitchen. Do not disturb.

THE SCIENCE BEHIND THE FUN

Growing sugar crystals is a great way to learn how saturated solutions are unstable at room temperature. The solution cannot handle any more sugar when the temperature falls, and crystals start to form. Over time, some water will evaporate, while solid sugar begins to crystallize. That's why it's important to avoid using a lid.

Sugar is a crystal with the formula $C_{12}H_{22}O_{11}$. That's a lot of atoms: twelve carbon atoms, twenty-two hydrogen atoms, and eleven oxygen atoms. They form as cubes, and their crystal "habit" is known as *cubic*. If

you measure the angles with a protractor, each elbow should be 90 degrees.

If you keep adding sugar solution to the jar, you can grow enormous crystals. This is a key to understanding how crystals form in the Earth. A solution that keeps flowing through cracks in the rocks will refresh the small crystals and they will keep growing. If you find small crystals in a rock, they probably didn't get a lot of time to grow. But large crystals usually tell mineralogists that growth conditions were perfect for a long time.

Grow your own perfect cube of salty perfection.

MATERIALS

- 1 cup (235 ml) of water
- 7–8 tablespoons (126–144 g) of table salt (sodium chloride, NaCl). Iodized is okay.
- Food coloring (optional)
- Piece of cardboard (optional)
- Clean, clear container
- Saucer (optional)
- 12″ (30 cm) string or fishing line (optional)
- Scissors (optional)
- Pencil or butter knife (optional)
- Paper towel or coffee filter (optional)

Safety Tips

- Don't get salt in your eyes.

- Wash hands quickly after handling salt.

- Ask an adult for help boiling the water.

- Be cautious around the cooking stove to avoid burns.

PROTOCOL

STEP 1: First make a seed crystal by pouring a small amount of saturated salt solution onto a saucer or shallow bowl. As the liquid evaporates, crystals will start to form, usually overnight. Select a single square crystal and remove it from the dish.

STEP 2: Carefully pour the saturated salt solution into a clean container (making sure no undissolved salt gets in), allow the solution to cool, and then hang the seed crystal with string in the solution from a pencil or knife placed across the top of the container. You could cover the container with a coffee filter or paper towel to keep out dust yet permit evaporation.

STEP 3: Set the container in a location where it can remain undisturbed. You are more likely to get a perfect crystal instead of a mass of crystals if you allow the crystal to grow slowly (cooler temperature, shaded location) in a place free of vibrations. It can take a week or more to get a big crystal.

Creative Enrichment

1. Experiment with different types of table salt and water. See if there is any difference in the appearance of the crystals.

2. If you are trying for the "perfect crystal" use un-iodized salt and distilled water. Impurities in either the salt or water can aid in *dislocation*, in which new crystals don't stack perfectly on top of previous crystals.

3. Make a mass of crystals by pouring the saturated salt solution into a clear container. Let it slowly evaporate. Crystals will grow on the sides of the container.

THE SCIENCE BEHIND THE FUN

The hardest part of this experiment is tying the thread around your seed crystal. But without the seed crystal, it's hard to get much more than crusty salt. The perfect seed crystal gives the extra salt in your solution perfect little places to attach to, and this is what will keep the crystal structure growing. This is the crystal lattice we discussed earlier. Salt has a perfectly cubic crystal lattice. It measures the same distance on all sides, no matter how big or small.

Salt is pretty simple. It has one sodium atom (Na) and one chlorine atom (Cl), clustered together over and over, to form a salt molecule. Thus the formula for salt is easy: NaCl. In the crystal lattice, the atoms repeat in every direction. Where there is a Cl atom showing, an Na atom can attach, and vice versa.

Salt is mined in many ways. In some places, solar evaporation of salt water produces salt crystals. There are also underground mines in salt domes where miners scoop up salt crystals or cut slabs of hardened salt into blocks. Some specialty shops sell salt from all over the world, which shows that salt is still an important part of our diet.

GEMMY GOODNESS

Grow your own perfect alum crystal, ready for shaping into homemade earrings or bracelets.

MATERIALS

- ½ cup (120 ml) of very hot water (boiling is okay but not required)
- 2 clean, 1 quart (946 ml), narrow-mouth glass Mason jars
- 2½ tablespoons (45 g) of pure alum powder (potassium aluminum sulfate—you must have the right kind!)
- Metal stirring spoon
- Paper towel
- Rubber band
- 12" (30 cm) of light nylon fishing line
- Scissors
- Ruler, pencil, or single chopstick

Safety Tips

- Ask an adult for help boiling the water to avoid scalding yourself.

- Avoid getting the alum in your eyes. If you do, rinse them with cold water.

PROTOCOL

STEP 1: Add ½ cup (120 ml) of hot water to a clean jar.

STEP 2: Slowly stir in the alum with the metal spoon. Add as much alum as you can until it starts to pile up on the bottom of the jar. This means your solution is saturated.

STEP 3: Cover the jar with the paper towel and use the rubber band to keep it in place. This keeps dust out of your alum solution and prevents impurities from wrecking your crystal structure.

STEP 4: Let sit overnight (sixteen hours minimum).

STEP 5: Pour the contents of the first jar into the second clean jar, leaving the residue in the first jar. Inspect this residue closely. These are small "seed" crystals that you're going to need to create a larger crystal, so make sure they are large enough to work with. If not, return the solution to the jar and wait another day.

STEP 6: Use the light nylon fishing line to tie a knot around the largest seed crystal. Do not damage the crystal. If it is too small, return to step 5 and get a larger seed crystal to work with. The more perfect your seed crystal, the better your end crystal will look.

STEP 7: Tie the other end of the line around a ruler so that you can hang the crystal completely in the alum solution. You can use a pencil or chopstick (or similar) instead. Do not let the seed crystal touch the sides of the jar or the bottom of the jar, as this will affect the crystal's shape.

STEP 8: Cover the jar again with your paper towel and rubber band. Place in a safe spot, out of the way where it can grow for many days.

STEP 9: Wait for at least a week. The longer you wait, the larger the crystal will grow. If you see small crystals starting to form on your jar, take out the crystal on the fishing line, place it back in the cleaned first jar, and pour the alum solution back in that jar as well (a fine screen might help). Don't let any of the small crystals get in, because they will compete with your big crystal for alum and it won't grow.

 Creative Enrichment

1. Try using thread and growing tiny crystals all along its length.

2. Try altering the cooling rate by adding ice cubes, setting the cooling jar in a bath of ice water, or keeping the solution in a saucepan and leaving it on the stove at a very low heat.

3. You could also grow a crystal without the string, just by letting it sit in the solution.

4. Try adding some glow-in-the-dark liquid from a yellow highlighter to your solution to make a crystal that glows under UV light.

THE SCIENCE BEHIND THE FUN

Scientists call alum a hydrated potassium aluminum sulfate, with the chemical formula $KAl(SO_4)_2 \cdot 12H_2O$. That means it has a potassium atom, K, and an aluminum atom, Al. It is a sulfate, which is sulfur and oxygen, and it is hydrated, meaning it has water molecules, in this case twelve, along for the ride.

Alum was used by the ancients to purify water, because it attaches to silt and solids, which either float or sink. Today, it is used to stop bleeding, in deodorants, and for pickling. It is known as *Fitkari* in India and *tawas* in parts of Asia.

Alum can grow into large isometric crystals that resemble two pyramids stacked at the base, if the solution gets refreshed. As long as fresh solution continues to flow into an area where crystals have started, crystals can grow. It is a simple crystal to grow at room temperature, and its faces can make attractive, inexpensive jewelry.

CRYSTAL CLUSTERS

Having one crystal is great, but that's not usually how the Earth works, and having a lot of them together is even more fun. Crystal clusters are a lot easier to enjoy, because you won't need a magnifying glass to see them, like you would with some individual crystals.

In nature, crystals usually form together because there is more than enough material. Crystals generally start as a liquid, and then cool down slowly enough to form proper "faces" on their crystal structure. Sometimes we get the right conditions to create veins, which can occasionally host rich zones of gold, silver, or other metal ores. In other conditions, these veins form small pockets of gems such as rubies, emeralds, and sapphires. A term you should know is *vug*—a pocket or gap in a vein where bigger crystals can form. Many of the most valuable gems grow in vugs, where conditions are often perfect to slowly form larger, better crystals.

CRUSTY CRYSTALS

Create your own crystals around whatever structure you think up.

MATERIALS

- Pipe cleaners
- 1-quart (946 ml) wide-mouth glass Mason jar
- 12" (30 cm) string or fishing line
- Scissors
- Ruler, pencil, or single chopstick
- 1 quart (946 ml) of water
- Borax, sugar, or salt
- Long wooden spoon for stirring
- Blue (or another color) food coloring

 Safety Tips

- Wash your hands after working with Borax.
- Ask an adult for help boiling the water.
- Be cautious around the stove to avoid burns.

PROTOCOL

STEP 1: Using pipe cleaners, create a framework of any shape—snowflake, square, pyramid, circle, etc.

STEP 2: Make sure that the shape can easily fit through the mouth of the wide-mouthed jar without having to squeeze through. If it can't, trim the sides down.

STEP 3: Cut a 6" (15 cm) length of string and attach it to one side of your pipe cleaner shape. Tie the other end of the string to a ruler, pencil, or chopstick. Make sure your framework hangs into the jar but doesn't come close to touching the bottom (leave about an inch [2.5 cm] of room). Once you have your length set, tie the knots and remove the shape from the jar.

STEP 4: Bring a pot with about a quart (946 ml) of water to a boil and pour about 3 cups (709 ml) of the hot liquid into the jar. Add 3 tablespoons (54 g) of Borax, sugar, or salt per each cup (235 ml) of water, so about 9 tablespoons (162 g). Stir it up, but don't worry if some Borax, sugar, or salt settles to the bottom of the jar.

STEP 5: If you want a colored crystal cluster, stir in some food coloring. You will have a little trouble seeing your shape as the crystals grow on it if you use a lot of food coloring. Now pour the mixture into the jar.

STEP 6: Use the string to hang the pipe cleaner framework in the jar, with the stick resting on top of the jar. Make sure that you've added enough solution to completely submerge the pipe cleaner.

STEP 7: Put the jar somewhere where it is safe from being disturbed. Leave it alone and let the science work without bumping it.

STEP 8: If you used Borax, you should have a nice cluster of crystals everywhere on the framework, and even on the string, by the next day. Sugar will take a little longer, and salt is the slowest (it could take two or three days).

 Creative Enrichment

1. **Try twisting your pipe cleaners into flowers, snowflakes, or other forms.**

THE SCIENCE BEHIND THE FUN

When you mixed the dry chemical with the water, you created a super-saturated suspension. A *suspension* is a mixture that contains solid particles large enough to settle out. By mixing the chemical into hot water, instead of room temperature or cold water, it stays suspended longer. If you used colder water, you would not be able to add as much dry chemical before it began to settle.

As the liquid begins to cool, it starts to crystallize. You'll see this crystallization on both the bottom of the jar and on your pipe cleaner. The solution continues to make a crust on top of your framework and on top of other crystals until you pull it out of the water.

Borax, also known as sodium tetraborate, is a term for a common salt with the formula $Na_2B_4O_7 \cdot 10H_2O$. The *B* is for *boron*. Borax forms from evaporation of boron-rich waters, especially seasonal lakes, such as in Southern California and Nevada deserts.

CRYSTAL GARDEN

The charcoal crystal garden is a classic crystal-growing project, because it's fun to watch grow. You can experiment with colors, too.

MATERIALS

- Charcoal briquettes, cardboard, or pieces of sponge or porous rock
- Glass dish or shallow bowl (non-metal)
- Hammer (optional)
- Water, preferably distilled
- 1-quart (946 ml) wide-mouth glass Mason jar
- Table salt (sodium chloride)
- Ammonia
- Laundry bluing agent
- Food coloring

Safety Tips

- Always wash your hands after using the chemicals.

- Get an adult to help you with the chemicals.

- The components of the garden are not edible, so adult supervision is recommended.

PROTOCOL

STEP 1: Gather your materials.

STEP 2: Place chunks of your *substrate* (i.e., cardboard, charcoal briquette, sponge, cork, brick, porous rock) in an even layer in the non-metal dish or bowl. You want small pieces, so you may need to (carefully) use a hammer to break the material up.

STEP 3: Sprinkle water, preferably distilled, onto the substrate until it has been thoroughly dampened. Pour off and discard any excess water.

STEP 4: In an empty jar, mix 3 tablespoons (54 g) un-iodized salt, 3 tablespoons (45 ml) ammonia, and 6 tablespoons (90 ml) bluing agent. Stir the mixture until the salt is dissolved.

STEP 5: Pour the mixture over the substrate layer (over the cardboard, brick, sponge, etc.).

STEP 6: Add and swirl a bit of water around in the empty jar to pick up the remaining chemicals and pour this liquid onto the substrate, too.

STEP 7: Dot drops of food coloring here and there across the surface of the garden. Areas with no food coloring will be white.

STEP 8: Sprinkle more salt (about 2 tablespoons [28 g]) across the surface of the garden.

STEP 9: Allow your garden to grow in an area where it will not be disturbed.

STEP 10: On days 2 and 3, pour a mixture of ammonia, water, and bluing agent (2 tablespoons [30 ml] each) in the bottom of the pan. Avoid pouring liquid on the delicate growing crystals.

STEP 11: Keep the pan in an undisturbed place, but check on it periodically. Let it grow until you are pleased with its appearance. Enjoy!

 Creative Enrichment

1. Bluing agent is found in the laundry aisles of some grocery stores. If you can't find bluing agent at a store near you, it is available online.

THE SCIENCE BEHIND THE FUN

This experiment combines the crystal growing methods we've been performing with a property of charcoal. Because charcoal is porous, it sucks up the water at just the right rate for the crystals to grow. The crystals are very delicate, almost dust. Use a magnifying glass or a hand lens to look closely at them.

2. The crystals grow quickly for this project because the substrate (charcoal or whatever you chose) has a large surface area. Crystals start to form on the porous materials and then grow as capillary action draws more fluid up from the dish. Water evaporates on the surface, depositing solids/forming crystals, and pulling more solution up from the base of the dish.

NEST OF NEEDLES

Build your own spiky crystals, atom by atom, so you can learn crystal structure.

MATERIALS

- Small bowl, mug, or disposable plastic container
- Hot water
- Metal stirring spoon
- Epsom salt
- Food coloring

 Safety Tips

- Wash your hands carefully after working with the Epsom salt and avoid getting it in your eyes. Epsom salt is used for medicinal baths, so it isn't bad for your skin, but it can irritate your eyes.

- Use warm, but not scalding, water.

PROTOCOL

STEP 1: Add ½ cup (120 ml) of hot tap water to a bowl, mug, or disposable plastic container.

STEP 2: Add a drop or two of food coloring.

STEP 3: Begin stirring in ½ cup (115 g) of Epsom salt with a metal spoon. (A wooden spoon will soak up the chemical, so don't use one. Plastic may stain, so avoid those, too.) Add the salt slowly. Toward the end, you may see that some salt going to the bottom of the container. This means the solution is saturated—the water cannot hold any more salt.

STEP 4: Put the container in the refrigerator for at least four hours.

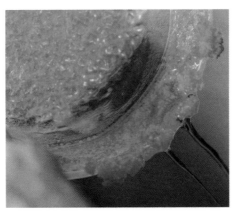

STEP 5: Remove the container and pour off any extra liquid. The longer you leave the container to crystallize, the longer the crystals will grow.

THE SCIENCE BEHIND THE FUN

Epsom salt has a chemical formula of $MgSO_4$—one magnesium atom, one sulfur atom, and four oxygen atoms. It gets its name from a spring in England, where people learned to soak in it to relieve aching muscles and joints. Today it is still used as a bath salt and in farming.

What is interesting about these salts is that they attract water to the point that it can be difficult to get an accurate measurement by weight, as the crystals constantly pull moisture from the air. What you're seeing in this experiment is rapid evaporation. Because you used hot water to hold your liquid solution of salt, you could saturate the liquid to the point where no more salt would dissolve. Once the temperature began to drop, the solution began to freeze. But instead of freezing like water, the solution crystallized more dramatically, sending spikes in every direction.

Since there are so many small, dissolved crystals in your solution, you don't need a seed crystal for the process to begin. Once water starts to evaporate, the salt crystals start growing. They build themselves from the bottom, so it's common to end up with a real nest of needles.

Unfortunately, these crystals aren't be used in jewelry because they break easily. They don't taste good, either. But this experiment gives fast results, so it's a great way to start learning about crystals.

Disposal of the crystals is easy: just rinse out the bowl. Food coloring could stain a plastic container, so it might be easier to rinse it and recycle it.

GEODES OF FUN

Make a cluster of geodes from common kitchen chemicals. This experiment calls for alum, but you can use Borax in the same proportions as the Crusty Crystals lab on page 22, or use salt in the same proportion as in the Salty Squares lab on page 16.

MATERIALS

- **Plastic eggs or small plastic bowls**
- **1 quart (946 ml) of boiling water**
- **Mixing bowl or 1-quart (946 ml) wide-mouth glass Mason jar**
- **2½ tablespoons (45 g) of pure alum powder (potassium aluminum sulfate—you must have the right kind!)**
- **Long wooden spoon for stirring**
- **Set of food coloring**
- **Superglue—don't use water-soluble glues**

 Safety Tips

- Avoid getting solutions in your eyes.

- Wash hands after using the chemicals.

- Ask an adult for help boiling the water.

- Be cautious around the cooking stove to avoid burns.

PROTOCOL

STEP 1: Make sure your plastic bowls or plastic eggs are clean. Note that you can also use actual eggshells if they are large enough, and *very* clean. Then you can break them away when you're done if your crystals are thick enough.

STEP 2: Bring a quart (946 ml) of water to a boil and pour about 3 cups (709 ml) of the hot liquid into a mixing bowl or Mason jar. Add 2½ tablespoons (45 g) of alum per each cup of water, so if you want to make a lot of geodes, keep that ratio. Stir it up, but don't worry if some alum settles to the bottom of the jar.

STEP 3: If you want a colored crystal cluster, stir in plenty of food coloring.

STEP 4: Put a few drops of glue in the bowl or egg, coating the inside edge. Before it dries, sprinkle in some alum, Borax, or salt crystals. These are the seed crystals that will help the geode grow faster.

STEP 5: Pour the mix into the plastic bowls or eggs. If you're using eggs, use a towel, a muffin tin, or empty egg container to hold the eggs upright.

STEP 6: Put the cooling forms somewhere where they are safe from spills.

STEP 7: After twenty-four hours, you should see a crust forming. It will take

some time for all the water to evaporate, but if you don't want to wait that long, you can pour the remaining liquid into a jar and reuse it for more fun later.

Creative Enrichment

1. Add fluorescent, glowing paint to your mix if you want to create a "space rock" effect.

THE SCIENCE BEHIND THE FUN

Geodes form in igneous and sedimentary rocks as hollow, round structures. They may begin as large bubbles or holes in the rock. Hot, quartz-rich fluids in the rocks can then reach the bubbles and start filling them in. Sometimes the hot fluids pick up colors from the rocks around them and leave colored agate bands inside the geodes. We'll learn more about that in Lab 42.

Geodes often look like ordinary rocks on the outside. Because they cool slowly and evenly, crystals can form into fantastic shapes on the inside. The geodes also get refreshed with new surges of hot liquid, usually quartz, but other minerals, such as calcite, may come in. Sometimes the new material comes into the geode

as a gas, so each crystal clinging to the inside of the geode can grow a little. Other times, the material comes in as a liquid, and the geode fills up with bands, from the bottom up.

Geodes and "thundereggs" are common in many parts of the U.S. where there is lots of lava, such as at Oregon's famed Richardson's Ranch. Keokuk, Iowa, is also known by rock hounds for its geodes. Cracking open a geode is a lot of fun, because you never know what's inside. There are many different websites where you can order your own geodes to break apart.

SPECIMEN SLEUTH

Now that we've built our own individual crystals and watched them grow in groups, it's time to study them. There are several tests that help set minerals apart, such as hardness, color, crystal angles, and density. By learning how to use these simple tests, we can narrow down the list of likely suspects when trying to identify something we don't know.

Using a system is important, because scientists have identified more than 10,000 minerals on Earth. Most are very rare, and some only occur under special conditions. More are discovered all the time, and it's still possible that you could discover a rare, unknown mineral and put your name on it. Try adding "-ite" at the end of your last name; if it sounds good, you can do an Internet search and see if it already exists!

The most common minerals that make up the Earth's crust have been known for a long time. If you can learn the basics about how to become a crystal detective, you can identify and investigate clues about the world around you.

LAB 8

SCRATCH THE SURFACE

Find as many items as you can and build a list of materials that can or can't scratch each other.

MATERIALS

- **Penny**
- **Pottery**
- **Porcelain tile**
- **Glass**
- **Nail**
- **Your fingernail**
- **A knife**
- **Crystals—pyrite, calcite, gypsum, quartz, etc.**
- **Lab notebook and pen or pencil**

 Safety Tips
- Sharp edges—don't cut yourself!

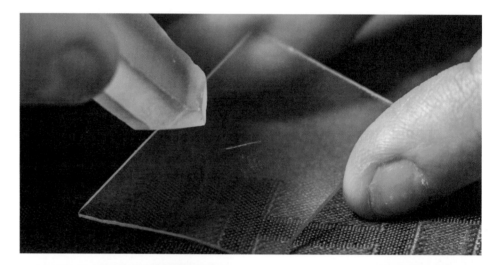

PROTOCOL

The idea here is to gather materials and try to scratch them. If you don't have any minerals, you can use things from around the house. Make a list and see if you can rank the materials by what they can and can't scratch.

Creative Enrichment

1. Try using a steel nail to scratch several different pennies—they are all a little different, but in general, older pennies are harder. Try other coins as well.

2. See if you can scratch a penny with a piece of glass or a different type of metal, such as a brass nail or screw.

3. Use a quartz crystal to try to scratch glass, coins, or steel.

4. Try other materials around the house, such as pottery, metal rulers, or older cookware.

5. Try scratching chalk, a penny, or piece of pottery with your fingernail.

THE SCIENCE BEHIND THE FUN

In 1812, the *Mohs' scale of mineral hardness* was devised by the German mineralogist Friedrich Mohs (1773–1839), who selected the ten minerals because they were common or readily available. The scale is not a linear scale, but it makes it easy to understand which materials are harder and softer. It runs from one through ten, with talc at one as the softest and diamonds standing alone at number 10—nothing can scratch a diamond.

Hardness is a function of a material's crystal lattice. Every collector needs to know the Mohs' scale, because it is an important field test. You can carry around a few common items and quickly zero in on a mineral's identification this way.

Notice how the fingernail is useful for comparison. Here's the list you should come up with from the lab:

YOUR LIST	
Mohs' Scale	Material Comparison
1	Talc
2	Calcite
2.5	Fingernail
3	Gypsum
2.5–3	Gold, Silver
3–3.5	Common pottery
3	Copper penny
4–5	Iron
5.5	Knife blade
6–7	Fine pottery
6–7	Glass
6.5	Pyrite crystal
6.5–7	Porcelain
7	Quartz crystal
7+	Hardened steel file

STREAKS OF MYSTERY

Learn how to use common porcelain tile to find the distinctive color of powdered minerals.

MATERIALS

- **Porcelain tile—a broken piece of white tile is perfect**
- **Various coins and/or metals**
- **Hematite (optional)**
- **Malachite (optional)**
- **Azurite (optional)**

Safety Tips

- Avoid scratching yourself with sharp porcelain edges.

- Avoid breathing in the powder you create on your streak plate.

PROTOCOL

STEP 1: Locate a clean edge on your piece of porcelain.

STEP 2: Drag the material you want to test across the porcelain and note the color of the powdered streak you leave behind. You may have to push down hard.

STEP 3: Test different materials, such as nails, coat hangers, and copper wire.

Creative Enrichment

1. What happens when you try to get a streak from an agate or petrified wood?

2. Is it possible to get a streak from a diamond?

3. What can you say is the science behind using a pencil on paper?

THE SCIENCE BEHIND THE FUN

There are two different principles at work here. First, porcelain is actually quite hard—about seven on the Mohs' scale. Thus, it is harder than most materials you want to test, and it will grind the material into a powder. Second, powdered material is "fresh," meaning it hasn't yet oxidized or weathered due to moisture, sunlight, or chemical reaction to water.

If you don't have the minerals listed, that's okay. You can still experiment with streaks using what you have around the house. Most metals are softer than porcelain, and produce a good streak. What happens when you find a metal that is harder than porcelain? You create a porcelain powder!

Most metallic objects like coins are a combination of different metals. Pure copper is too soft to make a good coin, so the mint adds strengthening metals to get coins that will stand up during circulation. Even gold leaves a streak (you can probably guess the color). Good jewelers can usually tell how much silver is present in a gold sample just from the color, which will be less of a golden hue and more gray or silvery depending on how much silver is present. But don't wreck good jewelry just for the sake of science!

LAB 10

BUBBLE TROUBLE

Learn how to make rocks fizzle. This is the classic "acid on limestone" test used in laboratories and field kits all over the world.

MATERIALS

- Lab notebook and pen or pencil
- Chalk—blackboard chalk is best, rather than sidewalk chalk
- Small plates or bowls, at least 4
- Lemon juice
- pH testing strips
- Medicine dropper or small spoon
- Magnifying glass or hand lens (optional)
- Vinegar

 ### Safety Tips

- Avoid getting vinegar or lemon juice in your eyes. Rinse thoroughly with cold water if you do.

- Do not breathe in the fumes that result from the chemical reaction.

PROTOCOL

STEP 1: Create a table or grid in your lab notebook to record your observations.

STEP 2: Put a small chunk of chalk in each bowl, all roughly equal in size.

STEP 3: Test the lemon juice for pH and record the results.

STEP 4: Add a few drops of lemon juice to a chalk sample and check for a reaction. Record your results. You may need a hand lens to view the reaction.

STEP 5: Test your vinegar for pH and record the results.

STEP 6: Add a few drops of vinegar to a chalk sample and check for a reaction. Again, use a hand lens to check the surface of the sample, if necessary. Record your results.

STEP 7: Repeat steps 4 and 6, but this time, crush the chalk into a powder first.

Creative Enrichment

1. If you have a piece of limestone, test it as a sample, and crushed up, with your two acids.

2. Try other rocks, such as dolomite and calcite.

3. Vary the temperature of the acid to see if that makes a difference.

4. Try different citrus fruit juices, testing each for pH and building on your grid.

5. Try grinding up a seashell and testing that.

THE SCIENCE BEHIND THE FUN

This experiment tests the science of chemical weathering, a significant force at the surface of the Earth. Your testing showed the relationship between pH and calcium carbonate, which is present in chalk, limestone, calcite, dolomite, and other carbonate-rich rocks. The fizzing you saw was a result of acetic acid (in the vinegar) and citric acid (in the lemon juice) attacking the carbonate, which is one carbon atom and three oxygen atoms: CO_3. When one of the oxygen atoms is removed, you create carbon dioxide: CO_2.

Acetic acid and citric acid are very weak, and thus safe for kids to use. College geology students studying mineralogy use hydrochloric acid (HCl) to perform these tests, resulting in a much more vigorous reaction. Field geologists often carry a small bottle of hydrochloric acid with them to test for limestone or dolomite. Limestone will actively bubble, while dolomite may require crushing or heated acid to produce a reaction. Common rocks such as quartz, agate, or basalt will not produce a reaction as they have no calcium carbonate.

Most surface water is slightly acidic and will slowly react with limestone and eat it away. This is why we see caverns in many large limestone formations. By constantly washing through the limestone, water can slowly dissolve the rock. The water then often carries so much liquid limestone that it will pick up the calcium carbonate and move it, creating stalactites, stalagmites, flowstones, and other formations.

LAB 11

CRYSTAL GEOMETRY

Learn how to determine a crystal's angle. You can even use the crystals that you made in Unit 1.

MATERIALS

- **Ruler**
- **Protractor**
- **Crystal samples, such as quartz, pyrite, calcite, feldspar, mica, or the alum and other crystals you made in Unit 1**
- **Lab notebook and pen or pencil**
- **Hand lens (optional)**

Safety Tips

- Avoid sharp edges on crystal faces.

PROTOCOL

STEP 1: Build a *goniometer* by placing the ruler at the center of the protractor, with 2 inches (5 cm) of the ruler extending below the protractor.

STEP 2: Place your crystal sample with one face along the bottom of the protractor, and one face along the ruler, so that you can measure one of the angles.

STEP 3: Record the various angles until you have a full set of measurements.

STEP 4: Repeat for different crystals, until you have built a full table.

Creative Enrichment

1. What other minerals around the house can you measure?

2. How can you measure pictures of crystals you find online?

3. A material such as obsidian has no crystal structure. Do you know why?

THE SCIENCE BEHIND THE FUN

The goniometer dates back to 1538, when it was described by Dutch mathematician Gemma Frisius, who was studying navigation and surveying. One of his students was Gerardus Mercator, who made a famous early map of the Earth called the Mercator Projection. Nobel prize–winning German physicist Max von Laue used a goniometer in 1912 to explore the atomic structure of crystals. Crystals have a distinctive, measureable angle to their appearance. No matter the size of the specimen, if you can measure its angles, those numbers should be the same whether the sample is as big as your hand or as small as your thumb.

Once you practice how to measure crystal angles, you can start to identify them by eye, without using a tool. For example, pure calcite crystals form a slightly tilted cube called a rhombohedron, with four angles on each two-dimensional face: 74 degrees, 106 degrees, 74 degrees, and 106 degrees, which add up to 360 degrees. Salt forms a perfect cube, with four angles of 90 degrees.

The next step is to learn to identify crystal habits—the common form a mineral adopts. There are seven common crystal habits: cubic, tetragonal, hexagonal, trigonal, orthorhombic, monoclinic, triclinic, and amorphous (no crystal structure, like glass). Once you start making a list of all the angles that you learn, you'll start to memorize them and then recognize them when you see them in the field. Geologists and mineralogists learn the angles and spot them even under a hand lens.

DIVINING DENSITY

Learn how to determine a mineral's density, sometimes called *specific gravity,* by measuring how heavy it is in relation to how much space it takes up. You can use your measurement as another way to identify a mineral, because almost every mineral has a slightly different density.

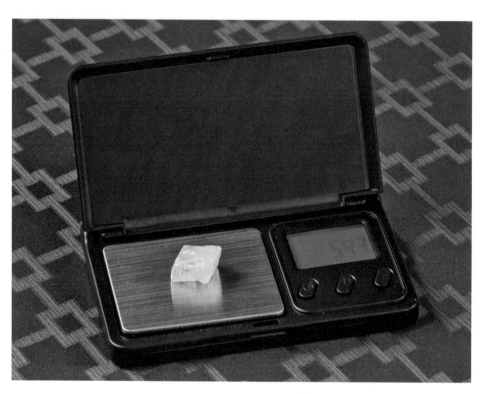

MATERIALS

- Small digital scale, up to 10.5 oz (300 g)
- Small mineral specimen, such as calcite or quartz
- Lab notebook and pen or pencil
- Small plastic container, such as a margarine tub
- Water
- Paper clip or piece of wire

 Safety Tips

- Don't cut yourself straightening or bending the paper clip.

PROTOCOL

STEP 1: Zero out your digital scale.

STEP 2: Weigh your specimen dry and record the weight in your laboratory notebook.

STEP 3: Fill your plastic tub about three-quarters full with water.

STEP 6: Suspend your mineral in the water. Do not allow the specimen to touch the sides of the tub or the bottom of the tub. Record the new weight.

STEP 7: Divide the larger number by the smaller number. Compare your specific gravity measurement against a reference such as the minerals database at www.mindat.org for your mineral and see how close you got.

STEP 4: Place the tub and water on your scale and suspend the paper clip in it, then zero the scale.

STEP 5: Wrap the paper clip around your specimen.

 Creative Enrichment

1. How can you measure larger objects?

THE SCIENCE BEHIND THE FUN

Mineralogists use a "key" to identify minerals, sorting samples by color, luster, streak, hardness, and density, among other characteristics. Field geologists use the term *heft* to guess density. If you pick up a rock in your hand and drop your hand a little, then raise it back up, you can feel how heavy it is naturally. But in the lab, you can get an exact reading that will let you compare against other rocks and minerals that aren't the same size. Density is a good thing to know, because a pure sample should have a characteristic density.

Density is mass divided by volume. The key to understanding density is that you are measuring weight for a standard volume: 1 cubic centimeter. The problem is that unless you are working with a cube or a rectangle, it's hard to use math to learn the volume.

Another way to measure volume is to put the sample in a measuring glass and see how much higher the water level moves. This is called *displacement* and it takes a lot of practice to do it right. When you are using very small rocks, the difference in the water level is hard to see. This lab makes it easy to measure density, even for small specimens—but you can't measure a mineral that will dissolve.

According to legend, the Greek scholar Archimedes discovered the concept of displacement when he got into a full bathtub and watched the water overflow. He used that knowledge to determine density.

LIVING WITH LAVA

Now that we understand a little about minerals in their crystalline form, we'll turn to some of the ways that the Earth uses minerals to create new rocks. Igneous rocks are the most dramatic way the Earth builds up its crust, usually in the form of lava flows and ash clouds. Geologists refer to lava as an *extrusive* rock, because it moved from inside the Earth to outside. Thus, extrusive rocks came out of the Earth. We'll talk later about the other kind of igneous rock, *intrusive* rocks that cool before they erupt from inside the Earth.

There are three main kinds of lava: basaltic, andesitic, and rhyolitic. *Basaltic* lava can be runny and form long flows that cover hundreds of miles or fill in gullies and valleys and end up several hundred feet thick. *Andesitic* lava tends to build up mountains, like in the Andes chain of South America. *Rhyolitic* lava is sometimes explosive, forming dangerous eruptions. All three help build up the Earth, but at this stage, you can use the term *lava* to mean simply "hot, flowing rock."

In these labs, we'll look a little closer at igneous rocks and learn more about their features.

VOLCANIC ACTION

The traditional volcano lab involves baking soda and vinegar, but that's not really a geology lab; it's a chemistry lab. In this experiment, you'll build your volcano the old-fashioned way: one lava flow at a time.

MATERIALS

- Small paper flower pot with a hole on top
- Several bottles of white glue or bottles of colored 3-D fabric paint
- Food coloring

 Safety Tips

- Don't get glue in your eyes, in your hair, or on your clothes.

- Don't squeeze the glue bottle too hard or you'll have a *real* eruption!

PROTOCOL

STEP 1: Select a paper flower pot with a hole in the bottom. You can arrange it on a board or piece of cardboard when you finish. You can use other forms for your mountain, such as Styrofoam shapes.

STEP 2: Prepare your lava sources (glue or 3-D fabric paint). If you are using white school glue, open the bottles and squirt a bit out. Then mix in plenty of drops of food coloring and stir or shake it up. Try to get at least three different colors for your lava. They can be realistic (dark brown, black, and gray) or you can choose a rainbow of colors.

STEP 3: Take turns reaching under the cone and squirting out lava from *inside* the flower pot, so that it flows down the flanks of the volcano, just like a lava flow. Let each flow dry for a few minutes before adding the next layer so they don't mix.

STEP 4: Work your way around and make sure the mountain is covered very well. When it starts to get messy, you can simply drip your flows from the top.

 Creative Enrichment

1. You can add some water to one of your glues to make it runnier.

2. If you want your mountain to look more realistic, try adding modeling clay or plaster of Paris to make a good crater at the top before you start.

THE SCIENCE BEHIND THE FUN

Volcanoes are the best understood source of igneous rocks. If you have looked volcanoes up online, you probably read about the 1980 eruption of Mt. St. Helens, which did not show us very much lava. Instead, Mt. St. Helens erupted with a giant ash cloud, as the lava inside rushed up and mixed with air too quickly to form puddles of hot lava. This happens more often than you think, and these explosive eruptions are very dangerous. Volcanologists—geologists who study volcanoes—call these kinds of mountains *stratovolcanoes.* These are usually snow-capped, nicely shaped, and pretty to look at, such as Mt. Fuji in Japan or Mt. Shasta in California.

Usually we get big lava flows from what's called a *shield volcano,* such as those in Hawaii. Hot lava pours out of these volcanoes in flows that sometimes go on for years, creeping along the ground and burning up everything in their path. Did you know that it is against the law around the world to try to interfere with a lava flow by building trenches, walls, or dams?

Other types of volcanoes that give us lava are called *cinder volcanoes.* They throw out a lot of ash and cinders, and build up a cinder cone. They are usually smaller and may build up on the slopes of a bigger volcano. Cinder cones also tend to come in clusters, with numerous little buttes and cones in a group.

INTRIGUING INTRUSIONS

This experiment shows how granite rises. When lava doesn't break through the Earth's surface, it cools slowly. We'll see how that intrusion gradually rises over time, like you would see in a lava lamp.

MATERIALS

- 1-pint (473 ml) wide-mouth glass Mason jar (or a drinking glass will work)
- 1 cup (235 ml) of water, room temperature
- Food coloring (optional)
- ¼ cup (60 ml) of inexpensive vegetable oil
- 1 teaspoon of salt (big, coarse rock salt works great)

 Safety Tips

- Avoid getting salt into your eyes.

- Don't knock over your jar.

PROTOCOL

STEP 1: Add 1 cup (235 ml) of water to your Mason jar.

STEP 2: Add four or five drops of food coloring and stir it in. This is optional, but it helps you see what's going on.

STEP 3: Add the oil into the jar. As you probably know, oil floats on top of water.

STEP 4: Sprinkle the salt into your mixture. It should drop to the bottom.

Creative Enrichment

1. Can you guess how much salt you could add before the mixture becomes super-saturated? Think back to the Salty Squares lab.

2. Does it matter what kind of oil you use?

THE SCIENCE BEHIND THE FUN

This simple take on a "lava lamp" is a little different from the original. The original uses a heat source that melts wax, which rises, cools, falls, and recycles itself. Other forms of this experiment use a lot more oil and effervescent tablets, such as Alka Seltzer, instead of salt. But they work on the same principle. Remember the Divining Density lab you did earlier? You can probably guess that there is a difference between the specific density of water and the specific density of vegetable oil. Most cooking oils measure about 0.92 g/cm^3. Pure water is defined as 1.0 g/cm^3. Since lighter fluids float on heavier fluids, the oil floats on top.

As you added the salt, it captured some oil on its way through the oil layer. This is because the surface tension of oil is high, so it wants to coat things, which you see as the mass drops through the oil. Once the salt reaches the bottom of the container, it starts to dissolve into the water, and as it dissolves, it releases the oil it captured. The oil then wants to rise above the water, and does so as an interesting bubble.

The difference in density is the same process that intrusions use to rise through the Earth's crust. They are just a little less dense than the material they are in, and hotter, so they rise slowly. Sometimes there may not be enough difference between the intrusion and the surrounding rock, so the hot magma eventually hardens in place, well below the surface. After a million years of erosion, or thanks to a continued push below, the granite eventually begins to poke out and form mountains.

LAB 15

LOVELY LAVA CAKES

In this lab, you will mimic what happens to a lava flow when it cools.

MATERIALS

- ½ cup (112 g) of butter
- 4 small custard cups
- Baking sheet
- Package of semi-sweet baking chocolate
- 1 cup (125 g) of powdered sugar
- 2 egg yolks—you might need help with this!
- 2 whole eggs
- 6 tablespoons (47 g) of flour
- ½ cup (30 g) of thawed whipped cream dessert topping, such as Cool Whip (or ice cream)

PROTOCOL

STEP 1: Pre-heat your oven to 425°F (220°C).

STEP 2: Smear some (not all) butter around 4 small custard cups and place on a baking sheet.

STEP 3: Microwave the chocolate and remaining butter in a medium microwave-safe bowl for 1 minute, or until butter melts. Stir in powdered sugar, egg yolks, and whole eggs. Mix well.

STEP 4: Add flour. Mix well.

STEP 5: Spoon the batter into your custard cups.

STEP 6: Bake for thirteen to fourteen minutes, until the edges of the dessert are firm. Remove from heat and let stand for one minute.

STEP 7: Run a knife around the edges to break the dessert free, and place them on individual plates. Many recipes call for you to turn the dessert upside down, but for this lab, don't do that. Don't sprinkle more powdered sugar on the top, either. Test the top of the crust just before you dive in—preferably while still hot—with the whipped cream. It should be like the top of a lava flow where the rock has cooled a little.

Creative Enrichment

1. Leave in a little longer to get the tops nice and crispy, like a real lava flow.

THE SCIENCE BEHIND THE FUN

These lava cakes show you what a real lava flow looks like, and why they are so dangerous: the top might look firm and hard, but the middle can still be hot and liquid. Unlucky tourists all around the world have been known to get too close to lava flows; the brittle crust breaks under their feet, leading to a fatal conclusion.

If you got the top of the cake nice and crispy, you should notice that it is quite a bit different in color and texture from the cake. That's because heat has almost turned the top of the lava cake to a cinder. The geo-logical term for that crispy top matter on a lava flow is *scoria*. It is usually full of holes and, in some lava flows, it may even contain little crystals of feldspar.

Scoria is different from *pumice*, a volcanic rock you may already know. Pumice floats on water and is much less dense. Scoria will sink.

Lava cakes are almost like a soufflé, and they may collapse when they cool. We'll talk more about that in the next lab, Collapsing Caldera.

COLLAPSING CALDERA

Some volcanoes erupt by belching out clouds of ash that blanket the land around them. Then they collapse and form a *caldera*—a large, circular crater. In this lab, you'll create your own collapsing caldera by making a soufflé.

MATERIALS

- 10³/₄-ounce (318 ml) can of reduced-fat reduced-sodium condensed cream of mushroom soup, undiluted
- 1 cup (115 g) of shredded reduced-fat cheddar cheese
- Electric mixer
- 3 eggs, separated
- 3 additional egg whites (total of 6)
- 2-quart (2 liter) straight-sided baking dish
- Cooking spray
- 1 tablespoon of fine dry bread crumbs

Safety Tips

- Use the usual safety precautions in the kitchen: avoid burning yourself on the stove or in the oven.

- Ask an adult for help using the stove and oven.

PROTOCOL

STEP 1: In a saucepan, combine soup and cheese. Cook and stir over low heat until cheese is melted. Cool.

STEP 2: In a bowl, beat egg yolks until thick and lemon-colored; stir into soup mixture. In another bowl, beat all six egg whites on high speed until stiff peaks form; fold into soup mixture.

Creative Enrichment

1. Some chefs use cream of tartar, sugar, or dried egg whites to stiffen the soup mixture and try to prevent the soufflé from falling.

STEP 3: Spoon into a 2-quart (2 liter) straight-sided baking dish coated with cooking spray and dusted with bread crumbs. Bake, uncovered, at 375°F (190°C) for forty to forty-five minutes or until the soufflé has risen and is golden. Once you take it out of the oven, pay close attention—the soufflé should start to collapse as it begins to cool.

THE SCIENCE BEHIND THE FUN

The truth is that almost all soufflés fall, sometimes within seconds of pulling them out of the oven. The beating of the egg whites causes air, in the form of tiny bubbles, to be trapped in the egg foam; as the soufflé bakes, the air expands, causing the soufflé to puff dramatically. When the soufflé cools, the air contracts, making the soufflé fall. But that's okay for this lab, because that's what we want. When you see a little wisp of steam rise and the crusty structure begin to sag in, you have created almost the same conditions as when a large volcano bulges up and then collapses. Only instead of a little harmless steam, *supervolcanoes* let go with a tremendous outpouring of volcanic ash, then collapse just like your soufflé.

Calderas can be quite messy. In the case of a caldera like the one in Yellowstone National Park, which is about 30 x 45 miles (48 x 72 km) across, geologists think that an eruption 640,000 years ago caused such an outpouring of ash that it circled the world and piled up several feet thick in parts of the Midwest.

Calderas may be some of the most dangerous geological features on the Earth, because they kick out a lot more ash than volcanoes do. People in Hawaii have learned to live with lava flows that move several feet in a day and creep downhill in predictable ways. Giant clouds of hot ash, on the other hand, can blanket entire states or even continents, ruin car engines, foul water supplies, kill livestock, cover farms and ranches, and block out the sun.

LAB 17

COCOA CRUST

Instead of just making hot cocoa on a cold winter day, make a model of how the Earth's crust moves around thanks to heat from inside the planet.

MATERIALS

- 1 quart (946 ml) of heavy cream
- Medium cooking pot
- 1 cup (86 g) of powdered cocoa

 Safety Tips

- Be cautious around the cooking stove to avoid burns.

- Ask an adult for help using the stove.

PROTOCOL

STEP 1: Pour the heavy cream into a medium cooking pot.

STEP 2: Cover the cream with a layer of cocoa, the thicker the better—close to 1/4" (6 mm). Make the edges around the pan walls slightly thicker. You just created a model of a "super-continent."

STEP 3: Turn on the heat and slowly bring the cream to a boil.

STEP 4: Watch where cracks form as the system gets hotter, and imagine how many earthquakes you could feel if you were standing on such a piece of the crust. See if you can predict which cracks will grow the biggest.

STEP 5: Keep heating, and avoid the temptation to stir. By the end of the experiment, you may be down to one remaining "island" of crust.

STEP 6: Don't waste the ingredients! Add a little sugar to make hot chocolate.

 Creative Enrichment

1. What happens if you make the chocolate layer ½" (1 cm) thick? Or use instant hot cocoa mix?

2. What happens if you use milk instead of cream?

THE SCIENCE BEHIND THE FUN

The interior of our planet is very hot—probably over 9,032°F (5,000°C) at the inner core, and ranging from 2,912°F to 6,692°F (1,600°C to 3,700°C) in the mantle. With all that heat and pressure, the rocks in the mantle don't behave much like rocks; they're more like plastic or toothpaste. That heat at the core of the Earth must go somewhere, however, and scientists believe it swirls around in currents through the mantle, just like the heat from the stove moved the heavy cream around.

As the heat increases, the currents in the cream scrape away at the chocolate layer that represents the Earth's crust, and finally, you started to see cracks begin. Wherever the crust was thin, the boiling cream found the weakness. At the end, you may even see the "plates" start to rock as the heat shifts them. At the Earth's surface, there are several rift zones where the rocks are pulling away from each other. These are *divergent* boundaries or zones where the crust is expanding. You should have also seen a "triple junction" where there were three lines of weakness and, eventually, the cream broke through. You could imagine that being a small shield volcano if the cocoa layer was hard enough for the cream to build up.

The theory of continental drift, also called plate tectonics, was first advanced by Dr. Alfred Wegener in 1912. However, it wasn't accepted until the 1960s.

SUPER SEDIMENTS

While igneous rocks can form in spectacular ways, most of the Earth's crust is covered with sedimentary rocks. Sedimentary rocks are named for the tiny bits of rock and mud—sediments—that build up when material settles out of water, including giant freshwater lakes and long, meandering rivers or active bays, lagoons, and straits in the deep ocean. Sometimes the water is muddy, and over the years, layer after layer of silt may settle out in a bay. Over lots of time, that *mudstone* can build up to thousands of feet or meters. Or a river may empty into the ocean and bring in lots of sand and rocks, creating *sandstone*. Elsewhere, a body of water may be carrying a lot of lime (calcium carbonate), building up until the water simply can't absorb any more chemicals. At that point, a *limestone* may start forming.

In this unit, we'll look at how sedimentary rocks get started and investigate some special forms of sedimentary rocks.

FUN WITH MUD

It may look like dirty water, but you'd be surprised how much is floating in there.

MATERIALS

- 1 quart (1 liter) of soil, dug from the garden—don't use store-bought potting soil
- Bucket and shovel
- Lab notebook and pen or pencil
- Scale (optional)
- Large, wide-mouth jar with lid
- 1 quart (946 ml) of water
- Long stick or paint mixer (optional)
- Screen or strainer (optional)
- Set of bowls (optional)

Safety Tips

- Avoid spills.

- Be careful where you dig to get your soil sample. Get permission first.

PROTOCOL

STEP 1: Collect your soil sample. Record the experience in your lab book: what you did, what colors you saw, how hard was it to shovel out, etc. You can find the weight of your sample by weighing the empty bucket first, then the bucket with soil, and subtracting the bucket's weight to find the final weight.

STEP 2: Fill your jar halfway with the soil you collected.

STEP 3: Add water almost to the top of the jar and put the lid on.

STEP 4: Shake up the jar and break up the clumps. You might want to take the lid off and reach in with a long stick to help things along. A long wooden stick used to mix paint works.

STEP 5: Return the lid and shake it up some more, then let it settle overnight. When you return, make notes about what you see. How did the material settle?

 Creative Enrichment

1. If you have a set of screens with big and little holes, keep going in this lab by dumping the contents into a tub and separating out the material. Put sticks, leaves, and other organic material in a container and put big rocks in another. Then measure out how much sand and clay you have and calculate the ratios.

2. Try the lab again, using a soil sample from another location.

3. Remember these skills for the Building Bricks lab. Save some of your soil sample for the Settling Sediment lab.

THE SCIENCE BEHIND THE FUN

Soil types depend on how much sand, clay, and organic material is present. Soil scientists do not use the word *dirt*. They either use the word *soil* or they use even more precise terms, like sandy loam and *alluvium*. By noting how much of each main ingredient is present, scientists can tell gardeners and farmers how to treat their soil with the right fertilizer. One handy tool they use is the Silt-Sand-Clay triangle, based on those ratios.

Did you find many big rocks in your sample? Chances are that you didn't. Gardeners like to remove big rocks. How about sand? Was there very much sand in your sample? Usually there is, and you can divide up the sand particles into fine, very fine, coarse, and very coarse. Measuring the size of the sand is usually something you need many specialized screens for, but it is

an important thing to know if you are a soil scientist. The first scale for classifying sediment sizes was developed by American sedimentary scientist J.A. Udden, and was adapted by C.K. Wentworth in 1922.

SEDIMENT SIZES	
Type	**Size**
Clay	0.0001–0.002 mm
Silt	0.002–0.05 mm
Sand	0.05–2 mm
Granule	2–4 mm ($^8/_{100}$"–$^2/_{10}$")
Pebble	4–64 mm ($^2/_{10}$"–2½")
Cobble	64–256 mm (2½"–10")
Boulder	256 mm (10")

SETTLING SEDIMENT

This lab shows how very fine silt and clay settles out until the water becomes clear again.

MATERIALS

- Soil sample (you can use your Fun with Mud sample if you have it)
- 3 large, wide-mouth Mason jars
- Water
- Screen (optional)
- Coin
- Lab notebook and pen or pencil
- Spoon

Safety Tips

- Avoid making a mess.

PROTOCOL

STEP 1: If you still have the soil sample from the Fun with Mud lab, you can use it here. Or you can get another sample. Place it in a jar and fill halfway with water.

STEP 2: Pour only the muddy water into the second jar. If someone holds a screen you can be sure to keep out big pieces of sand and rock.

STEP 3: Place a coin inside your third glass jar and pour in the "dirty water" sample you just made until you are almost to the top of the glass jar. Leave the lid off and allow for evaporation.

STEP 4: Write down your observations. What color is the water? Can you see the coin?

STEP 5: Over the next several hours and days, record more observations. You can use a camera to record each step. If the coin is still showing, you can prepare another "dirty water" sample and pour it in slowly; try not to disturb the sediments that have already settled out. You can do this by pouring your dirty water onto the back of a spoon held just above the surface of the water.

Creative Enrichment

1. Use a seashell to show how sedimentation can help make a fossil.

2. How many days does it take for the water to clear completely? Is the coin covered?

3. If you let the sample dry out completely, you might be able to pretend you are a fossil preparation expert and dig out the fossil from the dried mud.

THE SCIENCE BEHIND THE FUN

Sedimentation like what we saw in this lab occurs in many ocean bays and lagoons all over the world. There are three main kinds of sediment:

- **Clastic:** pieces of rocks and minerals and mostly sand and silt

- **Chemical:** different minerals that are suspended, like in the Salty Squares lab. When sea water is super-saturated it can no longer hold any more salt, and the rest begins to fall to the bottom.

- **Biochemical:** Many forms of sea life create shells to protect themselves. When they die, their shells sink to the bottom of the ocean, forming a calcium carbonate mud. The most common biochemical rock is limestone.

Since 70 percent of the Earth's surface is covered by water, there are a lot of sedimentary rocks formed by sediment simply sinking to the bottom. Over time, those muds and silts build up, and the weight of the water above them can squeeze them together. In the case of an inland sea, you could get thousands of feet of sediment building up over millions of years, but then earthquakes might drain out all that water, leaving only the hardened mud rocks behind. In other cases, you could have land that used to be at the bottom of the sea rise thanks to the way the plates of the crust move around. At some point, all those sediments would be left high and dry. Can you think of any other ways that sediments at the bottom of the ocean could become mountains?

LAYERS FOR LUNCH

Make your drilling sample out of a peanut butter sandwich.

MATERIALS

- Creamy peanut butter or some other nut butter if you're allergic to peanuts, such as almond butter
- Strawberry jam
- Marmalade jam
- Grape jelly
- 4 slices of white sandwich bread
- 4 slices of whole wheat sandwich bread
- Kitchen knife
- Lab notebook and pen or pencil
- Large, clear straws with a big diameter
- Chopsticks

 Safety Tips

- Be careful when using a knife!

PROTOCOL

STEP 1: Make four peanut butter sandwiches, and use *plenty* of jam for three of them, leaving the fourth sandwich plain, with only peanut butter. Mom or dad may complain that you're using too much jam or jelly, but it's okay—it's for science!

Creative Enrichment

1. If your straw isn't giving you good core samples, try straws of different sizes and materials, like a paper straw.

2. Try different types of bread or try toasting the bread. Does it help?

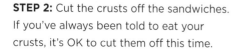

STEP 2: Cut the crusts off the sandwiches. If you've always been told to eat your crusts, it's OK to cut them off this time.

STEP 3: Stack the squares up on top of each other neatly. Record the order in your book.

STEP 4: Use your giant straw and "drill" a hole through the layers, turning it like a driller would to reach all the way through.

You may have to grind it against a plate to get the "core" as clean as you can. If you have a big straw, you can do this more than once, but don't fill the straw, as it may be hard to get your core sample out.

STEP 5: Use a chopstick to gently push the core sample out and lay it sideways on a plate or chopping board so you can see the layers on their side.

THE SCIENCE BEHIND THE FUN

To search for oil and gas in the Earth's crust, geologists rely on drilling to poke holes and recover the rocks in the correct order. These drills work best in sedimentary rocks, which are usually easier to drill through, but the drill heads are so powerful that they can also cut through igneous or metamorphic rocks. The best rocks for trapping oil and gas are usually sedimentary rocks, which are sometimes porous and can hold petroleum between their grains.

In other areas, geologists are looking for structures like domes that trap oil and gas. If they find a hard layer of rock that won't allow liquids to pass through softer rocks, they try to build a map to show the size of the dome and where they can tap it.

Sometimes the geologists find layers that aren't flat. We already know that when rocks settle out to make mudstones, they are laid down flat to begin with. When the drill core reveals that the rocks are tilted, they know that there might be a fault beneath them. Faults are another helpful structure for trapping oil and gas, because the softer rocks might suddenly find themselves lying next to harder rocks, which traps the movement of liquids.

Geologists learn a lot about the structure of the rocks beneath them by drilling. In the 1970s, Russian scientists started to drill the deepest hole in the Earth—the Kola Superdeep Borehole—which reaches more than 7.5 miles (12 km) down. It took them twenty-four years.

TASTY CONGLOMERATE

Make sedimentary rocks with your favorite ingredients. This is a *conglomerate*— a collection of bits and pieces of material, all glued together.

MATERIALS

- **Mixing bowl**
- **2 cups (312 g) of oats**
- **1 cup (25 g) of puffed rice cereal, such as Rice Krispies**
- **½ cup (50 g) of pretzels, chopped up**
- **¼ cup (42 g) of tiny candy shell-covered chocolates, such as M&M's Minis**
- **Medium saucepan**
- **¼ cup (55g) of butter**
- **¼ cup (85 g) of honey**
- **¼ cup (65 g) of creamy peanut butter**
- **¼ cup (60 g) of brown sugar**
- **Wooden spoon or firm rubber spatula**
- **1 teaspoon (5 ml) of vanilla extract**
- **Glass baking dish**
- **Parchment paper**

 Safety Tips

- Be careful with glass mixing bowls.

- Ask an adult for help using the stove.

PROTOCOL

STEP 1: In a large bowl, mix your oats, puffed rice, pretzels, and mini candies. Note that the ingredients list can vary depending on what you like—you can substitute cashews, raisins, chocolate chips, bigger candies, etc. Just keep the proportions about the same. This mixture will be your *clasts*.

STEP 2: In a medium saucepan, melt the "glue" for your conglomerate. Add the butter, honey, peanut butter, and brown sugar and bring it to a boil. Stir continuously so it doesn't stick. Reduce the heat and let it simmer for three minutes and keep stirring. Remove from the heat and add the vanilla.

STEP 3: Add the glue, or *matrix*, to your clasts in the large mixing bowl and stir together until you have everything distributed throughout the mixture.

STEP 4: Line the glass baking dish with parchment paper and add your mixture. Pack it down with your wooden spoon or rubber spatula so that it is nice and flat and even. You can add more candy, raisins, nuts, etc., at this point, either sprinkling them on top or pushing them in slightly.

STEP 5: Put in the refrigerator for about ten minutes, then remove and cut into squares or rectangles. Enjoy!

Creative Enrichment
1. **Is it possible to have too many pieces of candy?**

THE SCIENCE BEHIND THE FUN

Conglomerates are common sedimentary rocks. They are usually composed of rounded pebbles of various sizes but at least 2 mm (⁸⁄₁₀₀") in diameter or else they're just coarse sandstone. Sometimes conglomerates are glued together with such a hard, lime-rich matrix that they are very hard to break apart. Other times, they have way more rocky material (clasts) than they do matrix, and they crumble apart easily.

It takes very strong water current to move big rocks, and the size of the rocks in a conglomerate tells geologists a few things about where the conglomerate was made. If the pebbles and cobbles are not very eroded, they will still have sharp angles and corners, and the resulting rock is called a *breccia*. This usually means that the rocks have not traveled very far, and the water current when they were laid down was not very strong.

Gold miners often have to break up conglomerates to wash the gold out. Generally, the bigger the rocks in a stream, the bigger the gold. Conglomerates with large rocks in gold country are often a good sign!

MAJOR METAMORPHOSIS

In the labs so far, we have learned about the two main ways that new rocks form, through fire and water. But there is a third type of rock: *metamorphic*. These rocks start out as a volcano or a sediment, but undergo so much "cooking" deep inside the Earth that they change. Sometimes they change in profound and interesting ways.

In deep gold mines around the world, miners battle with the heat that increases as they dig lower and lower. We can only imagine what life is like for a crystal when it's buried under 20 miles (32 km) of heavy rock and heated up hotter than a pizza oven. We do know that under those conditions, crystals not only bend, twist, and fold, but they also change their chemistry. In the first labs in this book, we saw how crystals could slowly form under the right conditions of temperature and abundance. Things get even more interesting when you add pressure into the mix.

SMEARS OF PUDDING

Metamorphic rocks often look like swirls. This lab shows one way that might happen.

MATERIALS

- **4 different pudding mixes or 2 vanilla mixes with 4 food coloring choices—do not use instant pudding**
- **4 mixing bowls, with pouring spouts if possible**
- **Large glass baking dish**
- **Lazy Susan**

 Safety Tips

- Be careful around glass— don't drop it!

PROTOCOL

STEP 1: In the mixing bowls, mix the pudding ingredients according to the package instructions. You can use a mixture of dark chocolate, regular chocolate, butterscotch, and vanilla. If you don't have four packages of pudding, you can make two vanilla mixes and add food coloring to get different colors.

STEP 2: From opposite corners of your dish, quickly pour in two different-colored mixtures. Let them puddle out to halfway across the dish.

STEP 3: Right away, add two more colors from the same places you added them before. Pour slowly so the new pudding mix pushes the previous mix across.

STEP 4: Repeat as long as you have pudding mix, but for no more than five minutes, as pudding usually sets up within that time frame. Try to get nice, even lines in your dish that contrast well with the other mixes.

STEP 5: Before the pudding can set up, grab two opposite corners of the dish and give it a quick shake to one side with a jerk to stop it. This is where a lazy Susan rotating table can come in handy.

STEP 6: At some point, the pudding will set up and you won't get much more action. You can use a spoon or stick to make more swirls, but eventually the pudding is ready to eat!

 Creative Enrichment

1. What happens when great force is applied suddenly?

THE SCIENCE BEHIND THE FUN

Metamorphic rocks like schist and gneiss often resemble the pudding swirls you just created. Such rocks usually get their lines from the original strata in a sedimentary rock, which has been heated and pressurized by the forces in the Earth's crust. But earthquakes must also play a role, because the swirls and folds come in all shapes and sizes. When you gave your rocks a quick shake, you were doing the job of an earthquake.

If you were to keep going, at some point your pudding swirls would probably start to smear and become unrecognizable. Geologists believe the rocks in the Earth's mantle are very hot and probably act like pudding, or melted plastic, and as heat and pressure continue, the rocks change their appearance completely. In the lab Cocoa Crust, you learned about how heat travels through the mantle in convection currents, which can also cause melted rocks to form swirls. There is a lot we don't know about the rocks in the Earth's mantle, but this is a tasty way to learn!

SNAKY SCHIST

If sedimentary rocks are generally flat when they are laid down, how did they get so wavy?

MATERIALS

- **4 slices of yellow cheddar cheese at room temperature**
- **4 slices of white cheddar cheese at room temperature**

Safety Tips

- Don't make a mess with your cheese, but in this lab, it's okay to play with your food!

PROTOCOL

STEP 1: Take your slices of cheese from the refrigerator. Alternate colors of cheese to neatly stack five slices. Push the edges slightly so a rise appears in the middle. This is an *anticline*. If the bulge dipped down, you would have a *syncline*.

Creative Enrichment

1. Use a thermometer to record the actual temperature of your cheese samples.

2. What would happen if you spread mayonnaise between your layers before you start folding?

3. Try freezing your cheese and see if you can make a single fold. Some rocks are so brittle they don't fold—they fracture.

STEP 2: Take your stack apart and put three slices into one neat pile and the other two, plus one new slice, into another. Put the second stack in the refrigerator.

STEP 3: Holding the edges straight, make folds in the cheese by pushing the edges together a little bit at a time. You should see a mound form much easier this time. See how far it can bend without breaking.

STEP 4: Remove the second stack from the refrigerator and immediately repeat the experiment. Don't let the cheese warm up.

STEP 5: Make cheese sandwiches from your leftovers. Making grilled cheese sandwiches will turn the cheese into a metamorphic rock!

THE SCIENCE BEHIND THE FUN

When layers of rock get buried at great depths, they stop acting like rocks and start acting like, well, melted cheese. You can see how much easier it is to create folds when there is plenty of heat, because the cheese was much easier to bend. As the heat increases, you can almost fold your cheese layers like an accordion.

It should be easier for you to understand what happens not only to rocks the size of your cheese sample, but also to giant slabs of rocks that are heated up and pushed around. Geologists can tell how much heat and pressure a rock has been through by the minerals they find. If a rock gets more heat and pressure, it will become a slate, a common metamorphic rock. It may have started out as a mudstone but has hardly undergone any metamorphism. The next step is phyllite, and then schist. Finally, the rocks become gneiss, which is very hard.

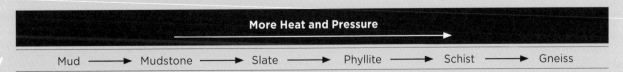

More Heat and Pressure

Mud ⟶ Mudstone ⟶ Slate ⟶ Phyllite ⟶ Schist ⟶ Gneiss

LAB 24

CHOCOLATE ROCK CYCLE

Use chocolate to learn about all the different rock cycles.

MATERIALS

- Block or chips of dark chocolate
- Kitchen grater
- Aluminum foil
- Small pot
- 2 cups (475 ml) water
- 4–5 paper cupcake holders
- Block or chips of white chocolate
- Chocolate syrup (optional)

 Safety Tips

- Be careful around a hot stove.

- Ask an adult for help using the stove.

- Don't hurt your fingers when you grate up the chocolate.

PROTOCOL

STEP 1: Start by making some "sedimentary" chocolate rock. Take a block of dark chocolate, or large chips—which you can think of as cooled "metamorphic" rock. Use a grater to grate about ¼ cup (44 g) of chocolate powder. This is like the effects of erosion, creating dry sand or mud—the basics of a sedimentary rock.

STEP 2: Create a small "boat" out of aluminum foil and place the powder inside it. Now float the boat in a small pot of water over low heat until you see the powder melt into a liquid chocolate lava flow. This is now "igneous" chocolate.

STEP 3: Pour the hot liquid chocolate lava into a paper cupcake holder and let it cool.

STEP 4: Once cool, break the chocolate into pieces, the way mountains break apart due to erosion. Grate some small shavings from the white chocolate, add it to the broken chocolate pieces, and sprinkle in some chocolate chips if you want. You can add some chocolate syrup, too.

STEP 5: Place the mixture of different types of chocolate "rocks" in a small square of aluminum foil, about 8″ x 8″ (20 x 20 cm). Fold the aluminum foil up by half several times until the chocolate is safely wrapped inside. You can also use sturdy resealable plastic bags.

STEP 6: Place the foil on a flat surface and push on it, but don't use too much force or you could break open the foil. You want enough pressure to press the chocolate particles together—like the amount of force needed to create metamorphic rocks. A light tap with a rubber mallet or a rolling pin would also work.

STEP 7: Carefully unwrap the foil and check out the result. You should see a "chocolate schist." By applying a little pressure, and some heat from friction, you forced the chocolate particles to compress together into a metamorphic rock again.

Creative Enrichment

1. **What could you do next to the "metamorphic" chocolate to re-start the cycle?**

THE SCIENCE BEHIND THE FUN

Congratulations! You just made a complete cycle through the three main rock types. There is no way to say for sure where rocks start in their journey, so we arbitrarily started with a metamorphic rock and began eroding it. Next, we melted the sedimentary rock and formed volcanic chocolate lava, then we mashed it all together like a metamorphic rock. If your mixture was hard enough, you could start over and begin grating it back into a fine powder. The Earth is a great at recycling rocks. That's the way it happens in the Earth's crust: rocks go through a journey from one form to the next. That's why we say that the Earth is geologically active—these processes are going on all the time.

BREAKING IT DOWN

Now that we've formed rocks in three different ways—igneous, sedimentary, and metamorphic—let's see how we can break them down. Every rock and cliff at the surface of the Earth faces big challenges every day, from sun, air, water, plants, and gravity.

You may not have thought about the Earth being an efficient recycler, but it is. Within seconds of a landslide breaking off from a cliff, the oxygen in the air will start to look for minerals it can attack. The wind will blow light material away, and the sun will bear down with heat and ultra-violet rays. Over time, even plants will get involved, using their seeds to find deep cracks where they can germinate and grow. In these labs, we'll learn how the Earth is always trying to recycle its rocks.

Scientists use the term *entropy* to measure how fast things fall apart. It is the nature of all things to eventually break down and disappear: Mountains rise and fall; plants and animals grow and die. Some processes occur quickly, out in the open, and some occur slowly, hidden from sight. In these labs, you'll learn why it is inevitable that rocks fall apart.

FINDING FAULTS

Use wood blocks to create your own fault and learn about some of the damage they can cause.

MATERIALS

- **2 smooth rectangular blocks of wood, sanded with no splinters**
- **Sandpaper, any grit**
- **Staples**
- **Marker pen**
- **Sheet of white paper**

Safety Tips

- Avoid slivers and splinters when working with wood.

PROTOCOL

STEP 1: Inspect your wood and make sure it is smooth on the corners. Sand down the edges if they are too rough.

STEP 2: Staple a strip of sandpaper on one side of each block so you can rub them together. It's best if you align the staples crosswise, so they don't scrape too far at once.

STEP 3: Use your marker to indicate the exact middle of the wood block and draw a line across the width of the block.

STEP 4: Face the wood sides of the blocks toward each other. Rub them together six or seven times and touch your finger to the wood where it rubbed. It should be slightly warm. This shows you how much heat can build up when wood moves only a few inches or centimeters.

STEP 5: Now place the blocks so that the sandpaper sides are touching, and repeat step 4. You should hear a scratching noise, and when you separate the blocks, you should see little bits of grit that fell off. This shows you how earthquakes can break down rocks.

STEP 6: Place the smooth sides of the block against each other, and hold one block in place. Move the other block a couple inches or centimeters to the left. This is called a *left-lateral fault*. If you move the block to the right, you made a *right-lateral fault*. These are called "normal" faults.

STEP 7: Place the wood blocks together, standing on edge, and tilted to one side at a 45-degree angle. Push one block up about 2 inches (5 cm). This is called a *thrust fault*. The edge of the block that you can now see is called the *hanging wall*.

Creative Enrichment

1. **When you moved the two blocks together without the sandpaper, did it shine up the wood a little? In the field, you would call this a *slickenside*. It's common where you find faults.**

THE SCIENCE BEHIND THE FUN

The structure of the rocks beneath our feet changes over time because the crust of the Earth is always moving. Structural geologists learn to see the Earth in three dimensions, and they know how to map a fault. Normal faults tend to be interesting at the surface, where rocks have moved alongside each other. Thrust faults are much more dramatic, because one rock pushes *above* another rock. In extreme cases, the faulting can be so unusual that the rocks completely flip, until older rocks end up on top of younger rocks.

When giant chunks of the crust bang into each other, something has to give. If they move alongside each other, like the San Andreas Fault in California, the motion along such a normal fault can be easy to measure and predict. Scientists at the U.S. Geological Survey have measured the San Andreas Fault moving about $2/3$ inch (1.6 cm) per year. It would be great if it just moved the same amount all the time, but during some big earthquakes, rocks at the surface moved many feet, and then the fault was quiet for a few years after that. Earthquakes can be difficult to predict.

SUNNY EXPOSURE

Watch the sun's rays fade images and make things look old. What does it do if it bakes a cliff all day, every day, for millions of years?

MATERIALS

- **Masking tape**
- **Cookie cutters, in various shapes and sizes. You can also use leaves, but you'll have to use tape on their back side to keep them from moving.**
- **Several different types of paper—newsprint, magazine pages, common printer paper, etc. If you can find sun-sensitive paper, that's the best to use, but it can be hard to find.**
- **Lab notebook and pen or pencil**

 Safety Tips

- Avoid direct exposure to the sun for prolonged periods, and always wear sunscreen—even on cloudy days!

- Watch out for hot surfaces.

PROTOCOL

STEP 1: Use masking tape to cover the cookie cutters so that the whole image acts as a stencil.

STEP 2: Place your different sheets of paper outdoors, then arrange the cookie cutter images so that you still have lots of paper exposed. If it's windy, you may also perform this experiment indoors on a windowsill, but direct sunlight is best. If you use photographic paper, keep it upside down until the last moment.

STEP 5: Continue exposing the paper to the sun as long as you'd like—up to three or four days, or even more. How did your predictions come out?

Creative Enrichment

1. Tape different materials over the cookie cutters and determine what effect they have.

2. Try as many different kinds of paper as you can find.

STEP 3: Note the time, and begin regular observations. Do not move the cookie cutters around, or else you will blur the lines. When you first begin, you might want to make predictions about which kinds of paper will react faster in direct sunlight.

STEP 4: After six hours, remove the cookie cutters and observe what is happening to the exposed paper and the unexposed paper. Take notes on color, how much sun is out, length of time, etc. If you used photographic paper, you won't have to wait that long.

THE SCIENCE BEHIND THE FUN

The sun not only beams light down on the surface of the Earth, but it also releases ultra-violet rays. Anyone who has had the misfortune of getting a sunburn knows just how relentless those rays are. Your skin has no good defenses unless you have a lot of pigmentation, and even that is not protection for most of us.

There are two ways that the sun helps break down rocks. First, there is heat. Under the rays of the sun, rocks tend to build up heat to a point where they can be hot enough to cause blisters when picked up. Heated rocks tend to expand, which can produce tiny cracks. When rocks heat up during the day and cool off at night, this results is a kind of push-pull effect where the rocks expand and contract continually, which can break down the chemical bonds that make rock-forming minerals.

Second, the streaming UV rays start a chemical reaction on many of the materials they reach. Combined with the tendency of water in the air to help oxidize materials, sun rays break down molecules and immediately begin to "age" whatever they touch. Like the paper you used in your experiment, the sun may dry out material, turn it different colors, or even burn off chemicals. The result is that the sun tends to age whatever it touches, and, while slow, it is still effective over millions of years.

LAB 27

RUTHLESS ROOTS

Watch sprouts break out of small enclosures. This shows how plants can help break down rocks.

MATERIALS

- **4 tablespoons (55 g) of mung bean seeds for sprouting—mung beans are a good, inexpensive choice, and they're edible**
- **Mixing glass**
- **Water**
- **Small saucer to act as a lid**
- **Big rock, about ½ pound (225 g)**

 Safety Tips
- Be very careful when mixing rocks and glass.

PROTOCOL

STEP 1: Place your seeds in the mixing glass, rinse twice, then add 1½ cups (335 ml) of water. Let soak overnight.

STEP 2: The next day, pour off the water and rinse the seeds. Don't let the seeds get slimy or stay too wet, but don't let them go thirsty for too long either.

STEP 3: When the seeds are near the top of the container, place the small saucer and the rock on top of them.

STEP 4: Monitor the seeds daily.

STEP 5: When it looks like all the seeds have sprouted, but they are still growing quickly, you can rinse them and toss out the seed husks and any seeds that didn't sprout. These tend to go bad quickly and can smell if they start rotting.

STEP 6: Keep rinsing twice a day as the sprouts grow.

 Creative Enrichment

1. What happens if you use an even heavier rock?

2. Do different seeds have different strengths?

THE SCIENCE BEHIND THE FUN

This experiment shows the force of a growing plant. By expanding and getting bigger, the seeds have the power to pop the lid off a container. Their ability to "push" is slow and steady, and they will keep going if they can. The other way that plants can break apart rocks is when their roots penetrate deep into cracks. The same general idea applies: the tip of the root is trying to find water or nutrients it can tap into, so it pushes and pushes until it comes up against something it cannot penetrate. Then it will try to go around, over, under, or backwards. While the tip of the root is pushing out, the root itself is growing and getting thicker. It won't be as delicate as the tiny tip of the root. The next time you go for a walk on a sidewalk, look at all the different ways the concrete slabs are pushed up or over by tree roots. You might even see cracks in the cement with roots poking up. That concrete never had a chance!

SHAKE AND BREAK

Rocks are very strong, but they can't last forever when they get rolled, shaken, stirred, and jumbled. In this lab, you'll mimic the forces that break rocks down into sand, and have a sweet time doing it.

MATERIALS

- **5 sheets of 8½″ x 11″ (21.5 x 28 cm) paper**
- **Pen or pencil**
- **2 boxes of sugar cubes**
- **Kitchen scale**
- **Hard plastic container with lid**
- **Selection of small pebbles. You can also use split shot fishing weights.**

Safety Tips

- Don't use a glass jar—it could break.
- Keep the lid on tight.
- Wash hands after touching the sugar so you don't make a mess or get it into your eyes.

PROTOCOL

STEP 1: Take a blank piece of paper and divide it into four quarters, or quadrants. Label the quadrants Boulder, Cobble, Pebble, Sand.

STEP 2: Place sixteen cubes on the scale and weigh them. Record the weight on your sheet of paper.

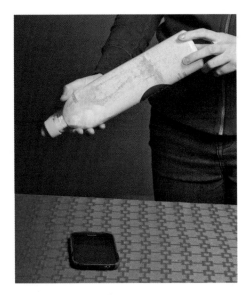

STEP 3: Place the sugar cubes in the container, put the lid on tightly, and shake vigorously for one minute.

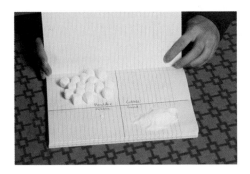

STEP 4: Dump the contents onto your sheet of paper and divide up the material. The largest chunks are probably boulders, and the finest material is sand. If you have tiny chunks of sugar that are almost broken up, call them pebbles. Cobbles would be the group that is too small to be a boulder and too large to be a pebble.

STEP 5: Weigh each section and create a table. Add up all of your measurements and see how close you get to the original weight.

STEP 6: Now vary your process. Try getting another person to shake the same number of cubes for one minute. Or you can repeat the test yourself and vary the time. Next, you can add a combination of rocks and pebbles or fishing weights and see if they change the way the sugar cubes break down.

 Creative Enrichment

1. How long do you think it would take for you to turn all the boulders into sand? Can you set up a contest with your friends and family?

2. What would happen if you put your sugar cubes in a smaller container, so that they don't have enough room to move around?

3. What happens if you put in the same volume of rocks and sugar?

THE SCIENCE BEHIND THE FUN

Mechanical forces that pit one rock against another are very common in the Earth's crust. When earthquakes move rocks over, under, or against each other, the result is often a pulverized powder. When rocks fall off a cliff and pile up below, the common term to refer to them is *scree*, as in a scree slope. Scree describes piles of rock that are mostly small. Geologists use the term *talus* (tay-lus) for slopes that are a jumble of large and small rock fragments. These may contain boulders the size of a car and are often not sorted very well, comprising a mix of huge, big, and little rocks. Each time another rock comes flying down, it will hit other rocks and break things down further. As long as the cliff above continues to be attacked by gravity, wind, sun, tree roots, and water, the talus slope will continue to build. Sometimes that's good—you won't have to climb the cliff to look for samples or fossils if they are always raining down from above. Just be sure to wear a hardhat!

LAB 29

FROZEN FORCES

Ice is another powerful force that can turn cliffs into talus slopes. One of the interesting things about water is that it doesn't behave the way you would expect when it freezes—it doesn't shrink, it expands. Think about when a wet storm dumps a lot of water on a cliff or rock. We know that water goes everywhere—into the tiniest cracks, making puddles in larger holes. If the temperature were to rapidly drop, that water would freeze and begin to expand. If there is somewhere to go, the ice will flow like toothpaste. But if there is no place to go, the ice turns into a very strong force.

MATERIALS

- Small balloons used for water balloon fights
- Water
- 1 empty 1-pint (475 ml) milk carton
- 1 cup (200 g) of plaster of Paris

 Safety Tips

- Don't use a glass jar—it could break.
- Use care cutting the milk carton.
- Wash hands after using plaster of Paris.

PROTOCOL

STEP 1: Fill a water balloon with enough water to make it about the size of a golf ball—about 2 inches (5 cm) across. Tie it off very tightly and set it aside.

STEP 2: Cut the milk carton in half and save the bottom half.

STEP 3: Mix up the plaster of Paris and fill the prepared milk carton to about 1/2 inch (1 cm) from the top.

STEP 4: Push the water balloon down into the carton and hold it long enough for the plaster of Paris to harden a little and keep the balloon where you put it. You want at least 1 inch (2.5 cm) of plaster of Paris above the water balloon, and you don't want it to touch the sides, either.

STEP 5: Let the plaster of Paris harden for at least an hour. Once it's hardened, remove the paper milk carton material.

STEP 6: Place the mold in the freezer and leave it overnight. In the morning, you should see cracks in the surface of the container. If your balloon was large enough, it may have actually cracked the block of plaster of Paris in half!

 Creative Enrichment

1. **What would happen if you left a lot of air in the balloon?**

2. **What would happen to a block of plaster of Paris that freezes without a water balloon inside?**

THE SCIENCE BEHIND THE FUN

This experiment simulates what happens to a rock cliff that gets water trapped inside the cracks. The freezing water expands, and since it is trapped, it cannot ooze its way back out. It can only push and push. If there is enough strength in the rock, it will resist the force as best it can. But even metal pipes can break thanks to ice. Any good plumber can tell you about water freezing in pipes and bursting the metal seams. These are called *atomic forces*—the physics behind water molecules lining up into ice crystals is happening at an atomic level. Most times, the ice finds a weak spot and the rocks survive. But over several storms per year, and millions of years, you can see how this mechanical weathering can be very effective.

LAB
30

READING RUST

Show how even common substances can break down a strong material, like steel.

MATERIALS

- 3 pieces of steel wool
- 3 plastic cups or shallow dishes
- Gloves
- Water
- 1 tablespoon (18 g) of salt

Safety Tips

- Avoid getting any steel wool "dust" in your eyes or on your skin.

- Don't get salt in your eyes—use gloves.

PROTOCOL

STEP 1: Place each piece of steel wool in a cup or shallow dish (wear gloves because steel wool can give splinters).

STEP 2: Pour equal amounts of water over two of the pieces of steel wool. Leave the third piece dry.

STEP 3: Sprinkle one of these wet pieces with plenty of salt.

STEP 4: Observe and compare the pieces every day for a week.

Creative Enrichment

1. **What happens if you use a copper scratch pad instead of steel wool?**

2. **What else can you use besides salt?**

THE SCIENCE BEHIND THE FUN

This lab shows you the power of chemical weathering. Even though it's made of steel, the steel wool you used isn't that strong up against acids and salt. By the time you finished this lab, you probably had nothing left of the steel wool but a gooey mess.

When the steel wool got wet, the water got right to work attacking anyplace it could find on the surface of the steel fibers. Any spare oxygen gas in the water began to attach to electrons given off by the steel to form iron oxide. This is called *oxidation,* and it is a very powerful force. There are many forms of iron oxide, but its most common form is red rust, with the chemical formula Fe_2O_3. That means there are two iron atoms (Fe, from the Latin *ferrum*) and three oxygen atoms.

When you added salt into the mix, you sped up the oxidation process. The reason is that the electrons from the iron can move around even faster in salt water. Salt water is a very good conductor of electricity for the same reason.

During the winter, many areas use salt to melt snow and ice before it can build up and make roads dangerous. You can now imagine the damage that salt would cause on the underside of your family's car. For that reason, some road crews use sand, cinders, or chemicals that are more environmentally friendly.

UNDERSTANDING THE EARTH

We started at the smallest scale, building up crystals and rocks and then breaking them back down. Now it's time to look at geology on a bigger scale. We live on a young planet; we know that because the continents are still moving, and volcanoes still erupt. Geologists believe that as planets get older, those forces stop. And yet it's an old planet as far as birthdays go—billions of years old. Once you can get those two ideas in your head *at the same time*, you can understand what is happening at the surface of the Earth on any given day.

In these labs, you'll get an understanding for just how old the Earth really is—measured in billions of years. Then you'll learn about some of the ways the Earth makes changes at the surface where you can see them. You'll also learn some basic geology mapping skills and how to mimic one of the most interesting geological events—the geyser.

LAB 31

MANY BIRTHDAYS

See just how old the Earth is and how hard it is to imagine the scale.

MATERIALS

- **Old deck of cards**
- **Glue (staples also work)**
- **Coloring markers**

PROTOCOL

STEP 1: Take an old deck of cards. Count out forty-five cards, which is all you'll need for this lab. Each card represents 100 million years, and you'll show how they correspond to the Earth's age, estimated at 4.54 billion years old.

STEP 2: Glue thirty-nine of those cards together into a single stack. Make it as straight as possible so the edges match up. Color these cards with brown edges. This group represents the *Precambrian* era—it covers the first 4 billion or so years of Earth.

STEP 3: Use a purple marker to color the edges of three cards. Glue them together and stack them on top of the brown cards. This represents the *Paleozoic* era. It lasted about 300 million years, so we round down to the nearest hundred-millionth place and use three cards.

STEP 4: Use a green marker to color the edge of two cards. This is the *Mesozoic* era, the age of dinosaurs. It lasted about 180 million years.

STEP 5: You have now accounted for all the time recognized by geologists except for the last 60 million years. You can round that up to 100 million years and place one final card on the top. Color it yellow.

 Creative Enrichment

1. **Can you think of a way to break up the last 60 million years to show the relationship if humans have been on the Earth for about 4 million years?**

THE SCIENCE BEHIND THE FUN

The Earth is really old—and not much is known about the early years. Geologists have used radioactive dating to measure the oldest rock known, a gneiss located in Canada, at about 3.9 billion years. The first thirty-nine cards in your lab deck represent a time on the Earth that we don't know much about. That's the brown zone of your deck. There aren't many rocks to study, so we have to make educated guesses about what the world was like.

By the time you get to the purple and green cards, we have more fossils to study and we know a lot more about the conditions then. But what about that yellow card for the most recent time? You could start over with sixty new cards, and color them to show the divisions that geologists use for the *Cenozoic* era. The current time is called the *Quaternary* period, and it started just 11,000 years ago. If you were to use one card for the Quaternary, you'd need 6,000 cards to divide up the Cenozoic era!

POLAR OPPOSITES

Play with tiny bits of steel and a magnet to show the North and South Poles.

MATERIALS

- **Iron filings or very fine steel wool**
- **Scissors**
- **Small (less than 20 ounces [591 ml]) clear plastic bottle, empty and clean**
- **Small test tube or plastic tube that fits in the top of your bottle**
- **Duct tape**
- **Magnets**

Safety Tips

- Use caution when using scissors to make your own iron filings.

Creative Enrichment

1. You can use magnetic black sands instead of iron filings.

PROTOCOL

STEP 1: If you don't have iron filings, take very fine steel wool and cut it up into extremely tiny pieces with scissors.

STEP 2: Remove any labels from your empty plastic bottle. Most water bottles will work. You may need a little rubbing alcohol to get the glue from the label off the bottle.

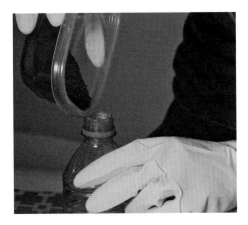

STEP 3: Add enough filings or cut steel wool to the bottle to fill it about one-fifth of the way—just less than a quarter.

STEP 4: Insert the test tube into the bottle and see how much space you have between the glass and the plastic bottle.

Remove it and add enough tape to make a nice, snug fit. Fully reinsert the test tube and slide your magnets back in. Put the cap on the bottle if you can or tape the top to avoid a mess.

STEP 5: Now you can play with the bottle. Try rolling it on its side so that the filings attract to the magnet. What do you see?

THE SCIENCE BEHIND THE FUN

Like the Earth, magnets work by creating a magnetic field with lines of force that come out of the North Pole and enter through the South Pole. The atoms in the magnet are all lined up the same, with the North Pole and South Pole always pointed in the same direction. In iron, the atoms aren't lined up, and point in all directions. Opposites attract: a North Pole of a magnet will attract a South Pole, but if you try to push two poles together that are the same, they will repel each other.

Magnetism is invisible, but the iron filings show you what the magnetic fields look like. The Earth works the same way, with a North Pole at the top, in the Arctic, and a South Pole at the bottom, in the Antarctic. When you lower your magnet into the test tube, the iron in the bottle jumps to the magnet and each small piece points in the same direction as the magnet. You can see the magnetic poles in 3D thanks to the bottle, and you should see little spikes at the poles. Once you remove the magnet, the iron will return to its normal state.

Geologists have learned that the Earth's magnetic field sometimes reverses itself, so that the North Pole is on the bottom. When NASA checked the regular lava flows that erupt along the ocean bottom, they found that iron in the rocks was frozen into place as the lava cooled. They learned that every 200,000 years, the Earth's poles flip. The flipping doesn't appear to hurt anything, which is essential. If we didn't have a magnetic field around the Earth, the sun's radiation would blast away our atmosphere.

AT THE OUTCROP

Make your own stratigraphic column—you'll change the way you look at cliffs!

MATERIALS

- Cliff face, such as a quarry or riverbank
- Lab notebook and pen or pencil
- Ruler (optional)
- Tape measure (optional)
- Camera (optional)

Safety Tips

- Find a cliff that is safe to access.
- Don't climb around or risk injury from falling rocks.

Creative Enrichment

1. In the photo on this page, calculate the thickness of each of the three rock sections, assuming that the car is 4 feet (1.2 m) tall.

PROTOCOL

STEP 1: The best way to complete this lab is to find a cliff, such as in a quarry or a road cut, made of sedimentary rock. Geologists call that an *outcrop*—a place where the rocks poke out from the soil. If you can't safely access an outcrop with an adult, you can probably find a photo online.

STEP 2: Estimate the size of the total exposure of rocks. Geologists do this with a tape measure, but you can hold a pencil out in front of you and slide your thumb so that what you guess to be the bottom 10 feet (3 m) on the outcrop relates to a couple of inches or centimeters of pencil. You don't have to be exact. Make a mental note of where the first 10 feet (3 m) ends, and move the pencil in your view to guess

1 meter (3.3 ft)
Soil, gravel

0.3 m (1 ft)
Peat

3 m (10 ft)
Sand, gravel

Hard pan
(unknow depth)

where the next 10 feet (3 m) ends. Do that again and again until you've estimated how many pencil sections fit into the whole outcrop. Multiply by ten (three, if you're using meters) to get the total number of feet or meters.

STEP 3: Sketch the outcrop into your lab book by making a tall rectangle or column. Put a zero on the bottom left and put the total number of feet or meters you estimated it to be on the top left.

STEP 4: Look for any horizontal lines in the rock face. These layers are called *strata*. Guess how far up the cliff each one is and make a line across the column in your book to match.

STEP 5: Finish your drawing and indicate the width that you guessed for each layer. If you don't know the names of the rocks, just use "red layer" or "black layer" or whatever makes the most sense.

THE SCIENCE BEHIND THE FUN

Stratigraphy, the study of how rocks stack up, helps you learn how rocks are organized even when they're underground.

Unlike the rings in a tree, rocks in a cliff face do not always show a complete record of time. There can be big breaks in time between layers; we call that an *uncomformity*. In some cases, earthquakes may cause shifting or erosion could wipe out a layer. In other cases, both layers might be flat and only a detailed study of fossils would reveal if there is missing time.

The study of rock layers dates back to Nicolaus Steno (1638–1686), a Danish scientist who laid out three basic laws: in almost all cases, the rocks on the bottom are the oldest; sedimentary rocks are usually laid down flat; and similar rocks found miles away are probably the same. In 1815, William Smith used those ideas to create the first geology map of a country, a giant colored display of England.

GUSHING GEYSERS

The classic "Mentos in a soda bottle" experiment shows one way geysers can work.

MATERIALS

- **2-liter bottle of diet cola at room temperature**
- **Sheet of paper, rolled into a tube to hold the candies**
- **7 Mentos candies**

Safety Tips

- Stand back! This lab can get messy!

- Avoid getting soda in your eyes.

PROTOCOL

STEP 1: Place the bottle of cola somewhere that is easy to wash down with a hose, such as a driveway.

STEP 2: Roll up the paper into a tube and insert the seven candies. Make sure the roll will guide the candies in quickly.

STEP 3: Place a finger over the bottom of the roll, and then position it over the soda bottle.

STEP 4: Release the candies and move away quickly.

 Creative Enrichment

1. You can adjust many variables in this experiment—temperature, flavor, brand, number of candies, etc.—to see what produces the best geyser.

2. Check the surface of the candy with a hand lens—what does it look like? What would happen if you took fine sandpaper and smoothed out all those pits before you try this experiment?

THE SCIENCE BEHIND THE FUN

When you drop in your candy, the carbon dioxide in the soda is immediately attracted to the candy surface. Because of all those pits in the sugar, your candy has hundreds of places for the carbon dioxide to form bubbles. These are called *nucleation sites*. This is similar to the experiments you ran when you created crystals out of salt and sugar. Only instead of allowing the seed crystal to slowly build up the crystal structure, you are starting a violent reaction as more and more carbon dioxide releases from the diet soda. If the candy is smooth, there are far fewer places for the reaction to begin, and the results aren't as dramatic. Another factor to consider is the weight of the candies—they are heavy enough to sink in the soda bottle and find more carbon dioxide to liberate.

If you use plain soda water instead of diet cola, you also get less action. Diet drinks have less surface tension, thanks to the artificial sweeteners, so there is less force to hold the soda together. If you imagine a large chamber of hot magma just below the surface, when the pressure is suddenly released, you don't get lava—you get an eruption of ash. There is enough air rushing in to mix with the magma and it turns into an ash cloud, rather than a lava flow.

Real geysers, such as Old Faithful at Yellowstone National Park, operate somewhat differently. Hot groundwater in a large void heats up rapidly to a boil, and then begins to rise quickly. If you were to try to conduct an experiment like that, it would be very dangerous and not nearly as much fun.

SIGNS OF LIFE

When we built a time scale of the Earth's age, we saw that our current geologic age is very young. But there has been life on Earth since tiny algae first started, almost 4 billion years ago—before there was oxygen in the atmosphere. Since we have limited rocks from those days, we don't have a lot of information about them in the fossil record. Still, we have enough to frame up solid ideas about what was going on.

In this series of labs, you'll look at all the different ways the Earth leaves us clues that we are not the only ones living here. You'll learn some of the different ways that the Earth creates fossils for us to enjoy, and you'll get to practice as a real paleontologist, gently digging away to get to something interesting. Long ago, geologists had some very unlikely theories about how fossils could end up on a mountaintop. Answering that question today seems easy.

LAB 35

PRESS A LEAF

Make an impression of a leaf—just like Mother Nature does.

MATERIALS

- ¼ cup (32 g) of cornstarch
- ½ cup (110 g) of baking soda
- ¼ cup (60 ml) of water
- Plate
- Wax paper
- Scissors
- 2–3 leaves or small branches; ginkgo and sequoia are excellent choices
- Diluted black watercolor paint

Safety Tips

- Keep all materials out of your eyes.

PROTOCOL

STEP 1: First, create your "fossil dough." Stir the cornstarch, baking soda, and water in a small saucepan and cook at medium heat until it forms a paste.

STEP 2: Remove from the stove and scrape it out onto a plate. After it cools, knead the dough as you would if you were baking bread.

STEP 3: Shape into six balls and put them in the refrigerator.

STEP 4: Cut six squares of wax paper, about 6″ x 6″ (15 x 15 cm).

STEP 5: Place a ball of dough on a wax paper square and smash it out so it is flat and round.

STEP 6: Press your plant material into the dough and remove it, leaving a fossil imprint.

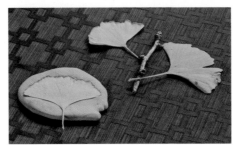

STEP 7: When the dough dries, you can lightly paint your impression with diluted black water color—just enough to highlight it—or you can use more paint as you wish. If you find your dough cracks too much, you can simply use modeling clay.

 Creative Enrichment

1. Look up the scientific name of the plant and label it in the dough by pressing with a toothpick tip.

2. What colors make the most realistic fossil?

THE SCIENCE BEHIND THE FUN

Most of the time when you collect plant fossils, you won't recover plant material. Unlike petrified wood, where the original chemicals have been replaced by quartz, a typical plant fossil is usually just an impression of the original. The black coloring that is common to plant fossils is usually some carbon that remained behind as the rest of the plant dissolved.

Gingkoes and sequoias are both a kind of "living fossil"—they are still around us after millions of years. The *metasequoia* is the state fossil of Oregon, but it's not very different from the sequoia trees that are common in California. If Oregon is cooler than California today but there are sequoia fossils in Oregon, what does that tell you about the climate when those sequoia fossils

were laid down? It must have been a little warmer back then.

By studying leaves, seeds, wood, and other fossils, we can learn a lot about the climate when the fossils formed. Geologists who study fossils are called *paleontologists*, scientists who study ancient life. As you can probably guess, studying ancient life means you must know a lot about present-day life, too, so you can make comparisons. Paleontologists are very interested in evolution—how plants and animals have changed over time to adapt to the changing world around them. Ever since the Earth could sustain life, about 3.8 billion years ago, the fossil record has left us clues about the world back then. Sorting it all out is like solving a puzzle, but it's a lot of fun.

Create your own dinosaur footprint. If you don't want to create a dinosaur footprint, you can use any plastic animal or real seashell. But, come on, dinosaurs are more fun to play with.

MATERIALS

- Mold container (e.g., small plastic cap from a water bottle, tuna can, etc.)
- Small plastic sheets
- Pre-mixed spackling compound, plaster of Paris, or other clay
- Dinosaur toy with accurate feet
- Nonstick cooking spray

 Safety Tips

- Clay can make a mess— don't do this lab on a carpet!

PROTOCOL

STEP 1: Make sure your plastic lid is clean.

STEP 2: Place a small square of plastic in the bottom of the lid so that you can remove the mold later.

STEP 3: Press in your clay, spackle, or other compound.

STEP 4: Spray the feet of your dinosaur toy with nonstick cooking oil. This will prevent any bits of clay from sticking to the toy.

STEP 5: Press the feet of the plastic dinosaur toy into the compound to make an impression. Make sure you get a strong, even impression. Check the dinosaur feet for bits of clay that still cling to the plastic; if you need to try again, you can spray more nonstick cooking oil lightly on the plastic and smooth out the clay to try again.

STEP 6: Let the mold dry completely; then remove it from the plastic cap. You can trim the edges, paint it lightly with a water color, or coat it with shellac. You can also put it in a bezel or attach a hook to hang it as jewelry.

STEP 7: You can experiment with common lids you have around the house.

Creative Enrichment

1. How would you create a complete track, where the animal's footprints record it walking in a line for a distance?

2. Measure how big your foot is in relationship to how tall you are. How accurate is your model based on that math? If your dinosaur footprint were 7 feet (2 m) long, how big would the dinosaur be?

THE SCIENCE BEHIND THE FUN

If you've ever stepped in mud on a sunny day, you've made a mold of your footprint. If the mud were to dry hard after several days, that mold could last quite a while. Now just imagine if a storm rolled in and the area was severely flooded, with a new, thick layer of sand, silt, and clay covering your tracks. All you would need is more flooding, more burial, and if enough weight built up over it, the mud would turn to rock and preserve your footprint for a long, long time.

The first dinosaur tracks identified by scientists were found in 1802 in Massachusetts. However, Native Americans created *petroglyphs* near several rec-ognized trackways in the western U.S., and these carvings translated to "location with bird tracks." The interesting thing is that the native people recognized the relationship between dinosaurs and birds long before paleontologists did.

Today, scientists can learn a lot about the dinosaur that laid down the tracks by measuring the depth of the imprint, the size of the track, and even the distance between tracks. There are places that seem to show a herd of dinosaurs all moving in a single direction, and there are sites that appear to show a predator chasing down their next meal.

CRAZY CONCRETIONS

Nature loves to coat things in mud and make them round—and big.

MATERIALS

- 1 cup (225 g) of unsalted butter, at room temperature
- 1 cup (120 g) of sifted powdered sugar, plus ½ cup (60 g) for rolling
- 2 teaspoons (5 ml) of vanilla extract
- Sifter
- 2 cups (250 g) of flour
- ¼ teaspoon of salt
- 1 cup (110 g) of finely chopped pecans, walnuts, or almonds
- 10–12 chocolate chips
- 1 cup (86 g) of sifted cocoa powder

 Safety Tips

- Be cautious around the oven to avoid burns.
- Ask an adult for help using the oven.
- Be careful when baking these tea balls—use kitchen gloves or hot pads.

PROTOCOL

STEP 1: Mix the butter and 1 cup (120 g) of powdered sugar in a large mixing bowl.

STEP 2: Add the vanilla and beat until fluffy.

STEP 3: Sift the flour and salt twice, and then add gradually to your butter mix.

STEP 4: Add the nuts and mix completely.

STEP 5: Roll the dough into small, 1 inch (2.5 cm), perfectly round balls, but be sure to push a chocolate chip into the middle. This can get messy! Place the raw balls onto an ungreased cookie sheet and cook for ten to twelve minutes at 400°F (200°C) until you start to see browning; then remove from oven.

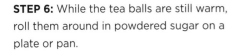

STEP 6: While the tea balls are still warm, roll them around in powdered sugar on a plate or pan.

STEP 7: When they cool, roll them around again, this time in cocoa powder.

STEP 8: Spray the tea balls with a water mist, and roll the balls again in powdered sugar. Repeat this step as many times as you can. The goal is to build a bigger and bigger tea ball, but after a while, it's hard to get any more powder on.

STEP 9: Cut a tea ball in half with a sharp knife, carefully avoiding knocking off too much sugar.

Creative Enrichment

1. Try just using water to build up your tea balls—does it work?

2. Try using an egg wash.

THE SCIENCE BEHIND THE FUN

Concretions are like nature's surprise—you never know what your prize will be. Sometimes there is nothing in there, but sometimes it's a fossil. You simulated the fossil by pushing in a chocolate chip. Many sedimentary rocks form in ocean bays or lagoons where the water is not clear and there is usually a lot of dissolved mud. When the mud is rich in calcium carbonate, it becomes sticky and begins to coat anything it finds. When you use dry powder, you don't have as much luck as nature does using mud, which tends to stick to everything, including itself. Concretions usually start by coating a shell, such as a clam or snail that was unlucky enough to get trapped there. This is the part you simulated with forming your cookie around a chocolate chip.

When small waves push around the small balls in this calcium-rich mud, the balls continue to grow, and can reach 6 feet (2 m) across. The famed Bearpaw Formation, which stretches from Canada to Colorado, was once part of the tropical seas. These rocks contain many deposits of concretions, which sometimes contain *ammolite*, a beautiful fossilized shell of an ammonite. These concretions are mined for their gems. Sandstone formations around the world contain concretions, sometimes with iron pyrite, barite, and other minerals. In 2004, NASA scientists using the Opportunity rover discovered small, round spheres on Mars, which they called "blueberries" because the rocks looked like a blueberry muffin. The spheres turned out to be rich in hematite, an iron ore, and the roundness was a clue that there was once water on Mars.

DIGGING FOR GLORY

Encase a treasure in a rock and remove it, just like modern fossil hunters do.

MATERIALS

- 4 cups (920 g) of plaster of Paris (or bucket of sand and screen for beginners)
- 1-quart (946 ml) plastic tub or a small ceramic plate
- 2 cups (475 ml) of warm water
- Teaspoon (5 g) of salt (for faster curing of the plaster)
- Sample "fossil" of your choice (e.g., plastic bugs or even a model dinosaur skeleton)
- Hammer and chisel or screwdriver
- Long nail, toothpick, or old dental tool
- Old toothbrush
- Safety glasses

Safety Tips

- Be careful when using hammers and chisels.

PROTOCOL

STEP 1: Determine how much work you want to make for yourself. (For young kids, or if you want to make something easy, you can simply use a bucket of clean sand and a small screen).

STEP 2: Mix plaster of Paris and pour it into a 1-quart (946 ml) plastic tub or a small plate. Add the salt if you want your plaster to harden faster.

STEP 3: Add your "treasure" (bugs, toys, or a model dinosaur skeleton) and stir in. Set the mix aside and let it harden for several hours. Thin plaster molds can harden in twenty minutes, but you just made a very thick rock.

STEP 4: Now the fun begins—pick at your jumble of parts and remove the plaster. A simple nail or screwdriver can help you poke and pick at the plaster, and a toothbrush will help you brush away loose plaster. It's fun to reveal pieces of your skeleton slowly and try to identify them before you get them out.

Creative Enrichment

1. Imagine how hard your job would be if all your fossils were delicate and broke easily.

THE SCIENCE BEHIND THE FUN

If you find that you have the patience to scratch away plaster and dig out your fossil replicas slowly and patiently, you may have what it takes to become a paleontologist. You'll have to get good grades and study geology, anatomy, and biology, among other things, to become a professional, but if you like to get out into the field, this is a great way to do it.

Hunting for dinosaur bones is a very popular vacation for some families—you can look online and find all kinds of trips all over the world. You'll get to spend time at an actual dig site and do many of the same things that the scientists do.

The western U.S. saw what became known as the Bone Wars, in the late 1800s, as soon as the wagon trains stopped moving across the plains. Doctors who went to medical school back east and moved their families out west quickly heard stories about giant bones, and soon, they went on family outings by horse and buggy to learn for themselves. Later, two scientists at big museums started a race to see who could discover and name the most new fossils. In his book *The Bonehunters' Revenge* (Houghton-Mifflin, 1999), David Rains Wallace tells the story of how Dr. Edward Drinker Cope and Dr. Othniel Charles Marsh started "the greatest scientific feud of the Gilded Age." They battled each other for years, trying to find the best dinosaurs first. Many of the top museums in the U.S., including the New York Museum of Natural History and the Smithsonian Museum still exhibit fossils dug up by these two men.

JURASSIC AMBER

Encase a bug in candy, just like the way amber encases fossil insects.

MATERIALS

- **3 tablespoons (42 g) of butter or margarine**
- **2 cake pans or cookie sheets**
- **1½ teaspoons (7 g) of baking soda**
- **1 teaspoon (5 ml) of water**
- **1 teaspoon (5 ml) of vanilla extract**
- **1½ cups (300 g) of sugar**
- **1 cup (235 ml) of water**
- **1 cup (235 ml) of light corn syrup**
- **Candy thermometer**
- **Package of gummy or plastic bugs**

 Safety Tips

- Be careful while measuring the temperature of the candy mix.

- Ask an adult for help using the stove and oven.

- Beware of choking hazards with the gummy or plastic bugs—especially if small children are participating in the lab.

PROTOCOL

STEP 1: Pre-heat oven to 200°F (93°C). Butter two cake pans and keep warm in oven. Mix baking soda, 1 teaspoon (5 ml) of water, and vanilla in a small glass and set aside.

STEP 2: Mix sugar, the rest of the water, and corn syrup in a 3-quart (3 liter) saucepan. Cook over medium heat, stirring occasionally, until it reaches 240°F (115.5°C) on the candy thermometer.

STEP 3: Stir in butter. Stir constantly until you reach 300°F (150°C). Another test is if you drop a bit of the mix into ice water and it forms strings. Do not burn the mix! Remove from heat and stir in the soda/water/vanilla mix thoroughly.

STEP 4: Remove the warm pans and pour the mix onto them. Place the gummy worms on the mix now. Or, if you want to more accurately resemble amber and bugs, you can set the bugs on the pans and pour the mix directly onto them, and place a few more on top.

STEP 5: Let the mix sit for about an hour to harden. Then break them out of the pan in big pieces. Store the pieces in a container with a lid.

Creative Enrichment

1. You can also do this lab using gelatin instead of candy if you want to cut down on sugar.

THE SCIENCE BEHIND THE FUN

It is possible to study insects, spiders, small birds, lizards, and other creatures trapped inside amber, which is fossilized tree resin—not sap, which has a lot more water. You may have seen a pine tree that has poured out resin when it has a deep gash or injury. When fossilized, the resin gets harder, clearer, and can take a polish, so it is used in jewelry. When rubbed, amber develops static electricity, and the Greeks called amber *elektron*.

There are several places in the world where people collect amber. In their book *The Quest for Life in Amber*, by George and Roberta Poinar (Addison-Wesley, 1994), the authors describe collecting trips to the beaches of the Baltic Sea, especially near Kaliningrad, which are still mined today. Baltic amber is often called *succinite*. Other areas where you can find amber include the Dominican Republic, Mexico, and New Jersey.

If you read *Jurassic Park* or saw the movie, you might remember that scientists searched all over the world for amber with insects preserved inside. The scientists looked for mosquitos that had died after sucking the blood of a dinosaur, and then they removed the DNA from the blood. It made for a good movie, but the chances of doing that aren't very good.

Not all fossils are big, giant bones. Geologists learn a lot from some of the smallest fossils, too.

MATERIALS

- **Chocolate candy bar with almonds, peanuts, rice, etc.**
- **2 plates**
- **Magnifying glass or hand lens**
- **Digital scale**
- **Dental flossing tool, toothpick, or nail**
- **Tweezers**

Safety Tips

- Be careful not to poke yourself while you dig out the chocolate.

PROTOCOL

STEP 1: Refrigerate your chocolate bar for at least an hour before you start. A cold chocolate bar isn't quite as messy, and the "fossils" pop out easily. You may want to stop and re-cool it if you start to get chocolate everywhere, or it may be easier to use warmed candy.

Creative Enrichment

1. Estimate the ratio of "fossils" to "matrix" before you start, then weigh your pieces after one section is complete. How was your guess?

STEP 2: Remove the chocolate bar and inspect it with your magnifying glass or hand lens. Look for the little "fossils" poking out.

STEP 3: Break off two chunks of the chocolate bar, weigh one, and eat it. You might as well get it over with!

STEP 4: Carefully begin breaking away the chocolate "matrix" using the toothpick or other tool and separate them out from the "fossils." Use the tweezers to set them on a separate plate from the chocolate.

THE SCIENCE BEHIND THE FUN

Fossil preparation is not as easy as you think, is it? You must carefully remove as much matrix as you can, and you don't want to break any of your pieces. If you've ever been to a major natural history museum, you may get to watch fossil preparation experts doing their job. One famous location is the La Brea Tar Pits in Los Angeles, California, where experts remove bones, seeds, twigs, and other material from the black tar. Even the smallest fossils help to figure out the climate when the fossils were laid down.

In this lab, you were picking apart a candy bar, but the crispy rice grains inside resemble a fairly well-known fossil called a *fusulinid*. These tiny creatures were single-celled organisms, but they grew a thick, hard skeleton to protect themselves. They were common from the Devonian to the Permian periods, but then went extinct. They are related to a group of small organisms called *foraminifera* that oil and gas geologists use to figure out the date of a rock they are drilling. *Forams* evolved into many different shapes and types, depending on the temperature and chemistry of their world, so geologists can figure out a lot about a rock if they know which foram they are looking at.

PROSPECTING FOR RICHES

It's time to get out a magnifying glass or a hand lens and look closely at what prospectors call *black sands*. These are the tiny dark specks in sand that can sometimes hold the most value. They are often tiny slivers of magnetite, but they can also be particles of iron, silver, platinum, or more exotic material. In rare cases, they may be star dust—tiny meteorites that fall to Earth. Tiny garnets are also commonly found.

Learning to identify and collect black sands can make you a good prospector. Any experienced gold panner will tell you that you always get black sands with gold, but you might not always get gold in your black sands. Another old saying that the prospectors shared was "gold is where you find it." What that means today is that 99 percent of the world's gold discoveries have been made, because the old prospectors were good at retrieving it from sites where it was most common. They would patiently pan many samples at the mouth of a river, and then work their way up stream, also panning the feeder creeks that led in. If they found gold in one spot but no gold above that spot, they knew to look right there for the source!

FLASH IN THE PAN

Learn how to use a gold pan just like the old-timers.

MATERIALS

- **Large, flat tub**
- **Soil or store-bought "pay dirt"**
- **Fishing weights, small lead split shots, or BBs**
- **Small gold pan—but a small aluminum pie pan will work**

Safety Tips

- Avoid splashing muddy water into your eyes.

- Rubbing your fingers into sand and gravel can scrape away skin.

- Don't pan for too long at first—you can get some sore muscles in your wrists, arms, and shoulders, or in your thighs if you squat down too long.

PROTOCOL

STEP 1: Fill a large tub about three-quarters full of water. If you don't have a big tub, a 10-gallon (38 liter) cooler will work. Don't use the kitchen sink!

STEP 2: If you purchase some "salted" pay dirt online, you can use that for this step. If you live near gold country, such as the Mother Lode region of California, you could visit a river and bring home a sample. Barring all that, use ordinary soil.

STEP 3: Fill your gold pan about halfway full of soil and add in the weights or split shot, if you don't have actual pay dirt. These are your "nuggets" and flakes.

STEP 4: Dunk the pan into the water carefully so nothing flows out. With your fingers, break up any clumps of dirt or clay, and if any sticks or leaves float to the top, remove them.

STEP 5: Let some of the dirty water pour off, but just a little bit. Stir the pan again and make sure nothing is sticking to the bottom. Swirl it around and make sure everything is broken down. This is called a "slurry."

STEP 6: If your pan has riffles, make sure these are on the far side of the pan. Shuffle the pan carefully so that everything in the pan moves slightly away from you, with the pan tilted down so just a little bit washes across the riffles and out.

STEP 7: Bring the pan back to level and swirl it around several times, then tilt the pan away from you again and slide the slurry against your riffles. Let a little bit slop over the top, then re-settle and do that again and again. Feel around again and make sure everything is broken up, and pick out any large rocks. Make sure they are clean—sometimes gold can stick to rocks, so be sure they are washed.

STEP 8: Again and again, swirl the pan while it is level, and then slide the contents of the pan away from you and across the riffles. Wash against the riffles until the pan is nearly empty—do you see a flash in the pan?

Creative Enrichment

1. Try another sample with the same weights in it and see how fast you can pan down to nothing but the lead shot.

THE SCIENCE BEHIND THE FUN

Gravity does your work for you when you use a gold pan. The old 49ers didn't have pans with riffles, so you have a big advantage, because the riffles create an eddy behind them and trap heavier particles under the lip. Every time you stop to resettle the contents in the pan, you do something scientific—you "re-stratify" the pan. All the heaviest material goes to the bottom, and all the lighter material rides to the top. This is because of three scientific principles—gravity, density, and water as a solvent. That's why every time you pan for gold, you are performing a science experiment!

If you remember the Divining Density lab (see page 40) where we measured density, gold is one of the heaviest of all elements—19.3 grams per cubic centimeter, when pure. Check out the chart on the right for the density of other heavy metals.

HEAVY METALS	
Metal	**Density (g/c3)**
Gold	19.2
Tungsten	19.4
Uranium	20.2
Platinum	21.5
Iridium	22.4
Osmium	22.6

BANDS OF BEAUTY

Use gelatin to create a banded agate you can eat!

MATERIALS

- **Mixing bowls**
- **Several types of flavored gelatin— 5 boxes will make 18 eggs**
- **Vanilla yogurt**
- **Egg molds—ask around, or try a second-hand store. Or use a common drinking glass for a mold.**
- **Nonstick cooking oil**
- **Syringe**
- **Whisk**

 Safety Tips

- Making gelatin requires hot water—be careful!

- Be cautious around the cooking stove to avoid burns.

- Ask an adult for help boiling the water.

PROTOCOL

STEP 1: Make your gelatin first. Dissolve a package of gelatin mix into 1¼ cups (300 ml) of boiling water.

STEP 2: Separate ½ cup (120 ml) of each flavor into a separate bowl and mix with 2 tablespoons (30 g) of vanilla yogurt to make it creamy.

STEP 3: Spray your mold or glass with nonstick cooking oil so that you can easily get the finished product out when you are done.

STEP 5: After each step, place the mold in the refrigerator to set for at least ten minutes. Don't let it harden, or your finished "agate" will fall apart along the lines. If the mix isn't set enough, the colors will run into each other.

STEP 6: Alternate your layers as you like them. The creamy gelatin may try to set on you, so use a whisk to fix it. Try to use the same amounts each time so your bands are nice and even.

STEP 7: Let the finished result set in the refrigerator for at least six hours. When done, the whole thing should come out easily from the mold. You'll know right away if your bands got too set along the way; try adding a little water and rebuilding them back in the mold and placing back in the refrigerator for a few hours to fix any accidents.

STEP 4: Fill the mold with different color layers. You can use a syringe to easily get the mix into the top of the egg mold if that's what you're using. An eyedropper also works if it fits into the hole. Don't make your layers too thick, or the banding won't look right. But if you make the layers too thin, you could be working on this project all day.

 Creative Enrichment

1. **How thin can you make your bands?**

THE SCIENCE BEHIND THE FUN

Agates are semi-precious gemstones that are made of quartz. *Gemologists*—scientists who study gems—call this mineral *chalcedony*. There are many different types of agates—mossy agates appear to have little fingers of minerals growing in them, and banded agates have lots of lines. Scientists believe the agate you made, usually called a fortification agate, is created when a cavity receives a little bit of liquid quartz at a time, over many, many years. Each band may represent another boost of agate material, or the cavity may have filled up all at once, and then settled out like we saw in the Settling Sediment lab on page 58. Each line may represent

time, or it could be small amounts of other minerals that have been carried along with the liquid quartz.

Picking up agates at the beach or along a creek or river isn't hard, but you need to know where to go. Basalt flows often have a lot of liquid quartz left over after the main minerals harden up, and those veins then travel along between old, hardened flows. Sometimes cracks in the flows will allow liquid quartz to travel up and down, too. The quartz eventually cools and hardens, and if it cools slowly, a beautiful seam of agate may result.

VUGS AND VEINS

Using cupcake mix and frosting, you can see how material is squeezed into the rocks in the Earth. And you can eat the result!

MATERIALS

- Cupcake mix
- Cupcake tin and paper cups
- Drinking glass
- Frosting (white or yellow)
- Frosting bag with nozzle
- Knife to cut the cupcakes in half

Safety Tips

- Be cautious around the oven to avoid burns.

- Ask an adult for help using the oven.

PROTOCOL

STEP 1: Prepare your cupcakes according to the recipe on a cake mix from the store or bake them from scratch. Don't make full-sized cupcakes—let them be about three-quarter size, or even half. If you're in a hurry, you can purchase cupcakes at the store, but look for smaller ones.

STEP 2: After the cupcakes have cooled, put one in the glass right side up and the other upside down so the sticky top layers meet. If you don't have smaller cupcakes, you can cut a big one in half.

Creative Enrichment

1. Try different materials, such as squeezing cheese in between two crackers.

2. Loosen up the frosting with extra milk or cream to make it runny.

STEP 3: Use prepared frosting to fill up a frosting bag with a long nozzle. Use white or yellow frosting to be more realistic.

STEP 4: Reach the frosting nozzle into the middle of the cupcakes. Push in a generous amount of frosting until you start to see frosting coming out in several places.

STEP 5: Examine the edges to see where your "vein" material appears.

STEP 6: Remove the cupcakes from the glass. If they get stuck, try again with another pair, but spray a little oil in the glass first. Once out of the glass, cut the cupcakes in half. What do you see? Think of this as a quartz vein that invaded a rock.

THE SCIENCE BEHIND THE FUN

In this experiment, you pushed a "vein" of frosting in between layers of cake, just like a vein might force its way in between layers of rock. Your frosting took advantage of the weak bond between the layers and may have also created veins in different directions or a "reservoir" of frosting in the middle. When these are hollow in the middle, they're called *vugs*, which sometimes contain valuable gem minerals such as emeralds.

Gold miners who rushed to the Mother Lode region of California first found gold nuggets and flakes in the creeks and rivers, but they soon turned their attention to the source of all that gold. They quickly traced the gold to a large system of quartz veins that they dubbed "the Mother Lode." These veins were squeezed into place along weak cracks in the rocks, often forced in between granite intrusions and the country rocks.

Geologists believe that when intrusions force their way up into the Earth's crust and cool in place, they often leave behind a liquid that is rich in quartz and other material. We saw in earlier labs that crystals form slowly in a saturated solution, but we used simple compounds of water and salt, water and sugar, etc. The veins in mining districts are much more complex, with lots of different elements. This residual liquid can contain iron, calcium, sulfur, and precious metals. The liquids often move around when earthquakes split open the rocks and create fresh cracks. Sometimes the veins form as small coatings at first, but the hot liquid may build up under repeated pressure. Other times, the veins may flow quickly into a crack and fill it all at once. A lot happens below the Earth that we can't see, but with experiments like this one, we can make a model of how things might occur.

SPACE ROCKS, TOO

One thing about geology—for the rules to work here, they have to work everywhere. There's no such thing as "European geology" or "North American geology." The same rules are assumed to apply on Mars and the moon, and so far, they do. We know the moon has lots of lava flows, and we know Mars has lots of iron-rich red surface rocks. Rules, after all, are rules.

We are learning more every day about the role of comets and meteors in Earth processes, and it makes sense that there shouldn't be a lot of mystery there. They are, after all just rocks. Fancy rocks, but still, rocks.

In this series of labs, we'll look at some of the processes we believe are at work throughout the solar system and beyond. And we'll look at impact craters and play around with how they form.

PRETTY PARTICLES

Use a common sparkler firework and show how streaking meteors can leave a wake of particles.

MATERIALS

- Sparklers and matches
- Small digital scale
- Lab notebook and pen or pencil
- 5'–6' (1.5–1.8 m) of white butcher paper
- Safety glasses
- Hand lens (optional)

 Safety Tips

- This lab involves fire and fireworks—you need adult supervision.

- If you have long hair, tie it back and out of the way.

- Do not wear any flammable clothes, such as a windbreaker.

- Do wear safety glasses.

- Have a garden hose nearby.

- Do not touch lit end of sparkler even after extinguished.

PROTOCOL

STEP 1: Weigh your unburnt sparkler on the digital scale and record the weight. Some of the ends may be hanging off the scale, but you should be pretty close. If you weigh several sparklers, you'll notice there is a wide variety in their weights.

STEP 2: Spread out your butcher paper on pavement, like the sidewalk or your driveway. Don't conduct this experiment on your lawn, as you could set the grass on fire.

STEP 3: Make sure all your safety precautions are in place—safety glasses, non-loose clothing, hose near. It's best if your hose has an attachment so that all you do is squeeze the handle to get water. Turn the faucet on first if you need it on to have water flowing.

STEP 4: Light the sparkler.

STEP 5: Walk slowly along your butcher paper as the sparkler burns. Notice the blackened ash that is building up on the paper. If your sparkler lasts a long time, you may have to walk up and down several times. Make sure all the sparkles flying off are landing on your butcher paper.

STEP 6: Once the sparkler is out and cooled off, weigh it and record the weight.

STEP 7: Once the ash from the sparkler has cooled, gather it all up into a small container. You might want to look at it under a hand lens, but weigh it first and record the weight.

STEP 8: Do some math and subtract what you have left from what you started with. Calculate how small of a percentage of ash you ended up with. Convert that to a ratio, so if the unburnt sparkler was 100 percent and the wire handle was 10 percent, what percentage of material ended up as ash?

 Creative Enrichment

1. **What if you could capture all the smoke that your sparkler let off—what percentage of the total do you think went up as a gas?**

2. **Where did the rest of the mass in the unburnt sparkler end up?**

THE SCIENCE BEHIND THE FUN

This lab shows that a meteor streaking across the sky leaves telltale clues. The weight of the ash from the burning sparkler didn't add up to much—probably less than a half gram. If your original sparkler started out at 1 ounce (30 g), the math works out to a residue of only 2 percent, and probably even less.

In science, the *law of conservation of mass* says that mass can't just disappear. Since heat doesn't have any weight, the only other place that mass could be is in the smoke. More accurately, the extra mass became a gas—smoke, carbon dioxide, carbon monoxide, and other compounds.

Scientists at NASA and the University of Washington have estimated that between 5 and 300 metric tons of space rocks, meteorites, interplanetary dust, and micrometeorites reach the Earth each day. Most of that material is in the form of micrometeorites, which contain organic materials, such as amino acids, and may be part of the reason there is life on our planet.

GUTTER MAGIC

In the previous lab, we looked at how shooting stars leave small amounts of ash behind as they burn up. Now let's see if we can find actual micrometeorites.

MATERIALS

- Broom or small hand broom
- Digital scale
- Lab notebook and pen or pencil
- Gold pan or deep metal plate
- Small plastic tubs
- Tub of water for panning
- Tiny sample jar (optional)
- Magnet
- Hand lens (optional)

 Safety Tips

- Avoid breathing in dust.

- Get an adult to help you if you are going to clean a gutter.

- Wear gloves to pick up garbage.

- If using a ladder, make sure someone holds it in place.

PROTOCOL

STEP 1: Determine how to find the small micrometeorites that fall from the sky all the time. If you live in an apartment, ask an adult to help you access your building's roof. If you live in a house, ask your parents if you can help clean the gutters.

If neither option works, sweep your driveway or a sidewalk. As a last resort, leave a big sheet outside with weights on the corners—some micrometeorites may fall onto it.

STEP 2: Collect your sample.

STEP 3: Weigh your sample if you want to; make more weight measurements as you go along.

STEP 4: Place your collected material in a gold pan or deep metal plate and begin picking out leaves, sticks, and other debris. Place unwanted material in your plastic tubs as you sort it. Any obvious man-made rocks such as bits of concrete can also come out, but inspect dark rocks to see if you think any have been burned. That can be evidence of heat while passing through the atmosphere. You may need to take such samples to a museum or school, but be prepared to hear the term *meteor-wrong*.

STEP 5: Pan your material down to black sands, as you did in the gold panning lab (page 112). Don't let any of your black sands get away this time.

STEP 6: Leave your black sands out to dry. Then use a piece of paper with a fold to funnel them into a small sample jar.

STEP 7: Use the magnet trick you learned on page 90 to separate out your magnetic sands. Inspect them closely with a hand lens or microscope and draw pictures of what you see in your lab book. What you're looking for are very round or oblong objects, perhaps pitted. Grains of magnetic sand that blow in are long and angular. You want the little round grains, as they are easiest to spot, but other material may be pitted with holes or have a black rim.

 Creative Enrichment

1. **What can you learn by measuring weight classes for the material as you work it down?**

THE SCIENCE BEHIND THE FUN

Collecting meteorites is hard. There are three main types: stony, iron, and stony-iron. You need to learn to identify a lot of features—fusion crust, flow lines, magnetism, and more. Geoff Notkin recaps all the key points in his book *Meteorite Hunting: How to Find Treasure from Space*. He uses an easy model to predict your chances of finding a space rock: every 10,000 years, a meteorite 0.4 ounces (11 g) or heavier lands on every square kilometer of the Earth.

Unfortunately, those iron-rich space rocks may quickly turn to rust, as we saw in Reading Rust (page 84). In the desert, where things don't rust so fast, you greatly increase your odds.

Scientists didn't even believe that rocks fell from the sky until the 1700s. Today, the most prized meteorites are the large ones, but smaller material rains down on Earth constantly, and some estimates say that 30,000 tons per year of "stardust" falls on the Earth.

A few online sources suggest leaving a big pan of water outside and checking it occasionally. Others use simple magnet systems, such as putting one on the outside of an aluminum gutter and another on the inside, where water can rush past.

MERRY METEORITES

Use marbles to watch what happens when meteorites blast out material as they impact the surface of a planet or moon.

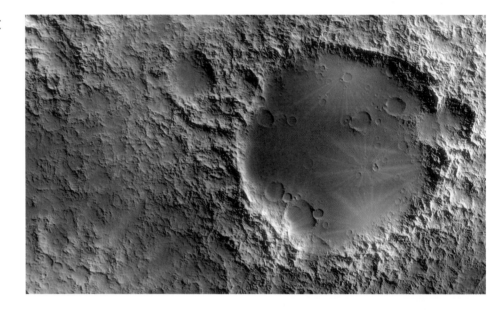

MATERIALS

- Butcher paper, magazines, or newspapers
- Medium baking pan or plastic tub
- Flour sifter or screen
- 4 cups (500 g) of flour
- 2 cups (172 g) of cocoa powder
- 1 cup (200 g) of colored sugar
- About 3–5 marbles of different sizes, or small fishing weights, or even BBs
- Measuring tape and ruler or meter stick
- Camera (optional)

Safety Tips

- Avoid making a mess—you might want to do this outdoors on the lawn or driveway.

- Don't throw anything so hard that you can't control it!

PROTOCOL

STEP 1: Spread the newspaper on the floor or on a table and place the plastic tub or pan in the center.

STEP 2: Fill the tub with sifted flour so that it is about 1 inch (2.5 cm) deep. Make it light and fluffy—don't smash it flat—and try not to have big chunks.

STEP 3: Using a sifter, sprinkle an even layer of cocoa powder over the flour. You can also swap the order of the layers to put the flour on top.

STEP 8: Continue dropping the rest of your marbles from different heights so that they each make their own separate crater. Observe and compare each crater.

Creative Enrichment

1. **What happens if you use a golf ball or a tennis ball?**

2. **What happens if you bring your meteor in at an angle?**

3. **How hard is it to resist the temptation to throw something bigger or faster into the crust model?**

STEP 4: Sprinkle a layer of colored sugar on top. Make it nice and even.

STEP 5: Select your first meteorite marble.

STEP 6: Using the meter stick, select a height and drop the rock into the pan from this height. Carefully remove the rock and observe the crater it made. Measure your results.

STEP 7: Without fixing the surface, select another "meteorite" and drop it from a different height than the previous one (but drop it away from the first crater). Compare this crater with the first crater and record the difference.

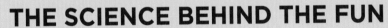

THE SCIENCE BEHIND THE FUN

From your experiments with different heights, sizes, velocities, and angles, you should have noticed that just about every impact crater ends up being round. The *ejecta*—the material blasted out of the crater—may go in different directions but the result is usually the same.

In 1902, mining engineer D.M. Barringer learned about a large crater near Tucson, Arizona, that was known to have iron rocks around it. Today, the Barringer Meteorite Crater hosts thousands of visitors each year. While trying to prove that he had discovered an impact crater, he set up labs just like this one to test the angle of the meteor before it hit.

Every planet and moon in our solar system has occasional meteorite impacts. Most impacts are very small,

but occasionally a giant meteor smashes in. Since the Earth is geologically active, with lots of erosion and earthquakes, we don't see many scars. But if you look at a full moon on a clear night, especially with binoculars or a telescope, you can clearly see some giant impact craters.

In their book *Field Guide to Meteors and Meteorites* (Springer-Verlag, 2008), O. Richard Norton and Lawrence A. Chitwood explain that the main asteroid belt lies between Mars and Jupiter, and most scientists believe those asteroids are the source of our meteors.

ROCKS OF ART

Now that you have learned more about rocks and minerals, it's time to go out and play with them. Ever since humans first started turning the things around them into resources, they have used the Earth's resources to their advantage, creating comfortable places to live by building shelters or stacking rocks to make fireplaces and walls, for example.

Rocks and minerals are also used for play and have been transformed into art objects, including using mud to create bricks and mixing materials to make paint. In these labs, you'll trace the steps that early humans took as they learned to make geology a greater, creative part of their lives.

MAKE MY PAINT

Ancient humans made their own paint from rocks, and so can you. They used *ochre*, a natural pigment in soil that is high in iron oxide (just like in the lab Reading Rust). Some regions have lots of distinct red or yellow soil to collect, but if not you can work around that.

MATERIALS

- Natural ochre if you can find it; or use chalk and a small grater (use powdered paint as last resort)
- Very small metal pot or small ceramic dish that won't stain
- 1 cup (235 ml) of water
- White PVA glue such as Elmer's or wood glue (optional)
- Flat board, rock, or paper to paint
- Paintbrush or flat stick, like a popsicle stick

PROTOCOL

STEP 1: If you don't have natural ochre, use a grater and sticks of chalk to make some piles of powder.

STEP 2: Add ¼ teaspoon (1 g) of powder to a used metal pot or small dish that you won't need for cooking. Most paint can easily stain plastic, wood, or certain ceramics.

STEP 3: Add enough water (or white glue) to the powder to create a runny liquid.

STEP 4: Apply the paint to a rock, a piece of paper, or a stick. If you want to mix up more colors, you can find or purchase more varieties of chalk, or find more ochre, and practice mixing them.

STEP 5: Let your painting set and dry completely.

Creative Enrichment

1. If you want to use the color black, try a piece of charcoal and crush it up into a powder. Use gloves. Do not use charcoal briquettes that are self-lighting—they can smell bad and give off fumes.

2. Think back to the crystals we made at the beginning of the book (see page 24)—what can you use for blue tinting?

Safety Tips

- Be very careful about staining your clothes, dishes, or countertops. Wear old clothes and set out old towels or newspapers to avoid making a mess with splashes.

THE SCIENCE BEHIND THE FUN

When we learned to identify rocks and minerals in Streaks of Mystery, we saw that many powdered minerals have a distinctive color. Some ancient tribes used water and red ochre to paint their skins red for special ceremonies. The mineral hematite produces a distinctive red powder, essentially iron rust. Some hematite deposits have completely disintegrated into beds of powder, and that's what ancient tribes used for red pigment. In other conditions, iron minerals turn yellow—another color source. Similarly, some copper minerals give a blue pigment when powdered.

The ancients often used minerals that are very dangerous, including arsenic and lead, to create vivid colors beyond red and yellow. By mixing powdered minerals with beeswax, butter, or sheep fat the ancients created cosmetics. Ancient Egyptians used a combination of burnt almonds, copper ores, lead, ash, and ochre—which they called *kohl*—to outline their eyes in a characteristic almond shape. Romans were said to use so much lead in their cosmetics and plumbing that lead poisoning was a big problem.

LAB
48

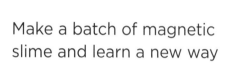

GLAMOROUS GOO

Make a batch of magnetic slime and learn a new way to play with magnetism.

MATERIALS

- **4 oz (118 ml) white school glue**
- **$\frac{1}{3}$ cup (80 ml) water**
- **2 tbsp (15 g) iron oxide, ferrous oxide, or magnetic sands**
- **Small bowl**
- **Plastic spoon or spatula**
- **Funnel**
- **$\frac{1}{2}$ cup (119 ml) liquid starch**
- **Strong neodymium magnets**

 Safety Tips

- Avoid getting the slime in your eyes.

- Wash hands thoroughly after using.

- Iron oxide makes a far bigger mess than magnetic black sands. You may want to wear gloves and use plastic sheeting to prevent stains.

PROTOCOL

STEP 1: Pour the white glue into the small bowl.

STEP 2: Use a funnel to add 3 oz (90 ml) water to the empty glue container. Swish it around in the bottle and then pour it into the bowl.

STEP 3: Add the iron oxide or magnetic black sands and stir until mixed.

STEP 4: Add the liquid starch and mix everything together. Remove the mixture from the bowl.

STEP 5: Use a strong magnet to play with the slime. You can place the magnet close to the slime and attract a long finger of material, or place a bar magnet in the slime and watch the slime cover the magnet.

 Creative Enrichment

1. **What other iron material can you use?**

2. **How well do ordinary magnets work with your slime?**

THE SCIENCE BEHIND THE FUN

By combining glue, water, and liquid starch, you created an interesting goo that is fun to play with. It can stretch out to a thin sheet and it's easy to make. The science comes in because you added iron to the slime. All of the properties of magnetism are still there to play with, just in a more interesting form.

If you place a powerful magnet near the slime, you should see a small finger of magnetic material start to extend toward the magnet. If you were to freeze the slime and study a thin section under a microscope, you'd see the iron oxide lined up along the slime's magnetic field.

As planets formed while our solar system was still young, magnetism was already a powerful force. So was gravity. We still have a lot to learn about how star dust and space rocks combine into dense planets in the vacuum of space, but scientists using the Hubble Space Telescope have observed some amazing things already.

BUILDING BRICKS

Use mud, straw, and wood to make your own bricks.

MATERIALS

- Clay-rich dirt
- 1-quart (1 liter) wide-mouth Mason jar
- Water
- Spoon
- Sand (optional)
- Silicone ice cube trays
- Turkey baster

Safety Tips

- Messes happen any time you play around with dirt and water. It's best to do this activity outdoors!

- Be careful using the oven and use oven mitts with the hot mold.

- Ask an adult for help using the oven.

PROTOCOL

STEP 1: For this lab, you need clay-rich soil that is sticky when wet. Mix up your sample and then let it settle, like we did in Fun with Mud (page 56). Add about 2 cups (460 g) of soil to the Mason jar. Fill the jar with water to within about an inch (2.5 cm) of the top and stir well, breaking up the chunks. Let it settle overnight. In the morning, you should have three separate bands of material: a thin layer of sand on the bottom, then silt, then clay. Ideally, you want a mixture that is about 30 percent sand and silt and 70 percent clay, but a 50-50 mix will work. Add sand or remove clay with a spoon to get the ratio right. Let it settle again.

STEP 2: Select a silicone ice cube tray to use as your mold. Make sure it is clean and free of holes, dirt, etc. A pastry mold also works.

STEP 3: Use a turkey baster to remove the water from the settled jar. If you pour the water out, you will stir the mix and lose clay.

STEP 4: Stir up the mix thoroughly. Pour or spoon the clay mixture into your ice cube tray and remove any rocks or twigs.

STEP 5: Bake the mold in the oven at 150°F (65.5°C) for four hours. If there was a lot of water in the mix, remove the tray from the oven halfway through and use a spoon to push the edges of the brick back into place. When the bricks are hard, remove from the oven and let cool. Free the bricks by flipping over the mold and tapping it lightly.

STEP 6: Dry the bricks on a paper towel. After an hour, turn them on their edges to dry some more. This whole process will take a day or two. The final moisture content of the adobe clay brick will be around 10 or 15 percent. At this point, the adobe bricks will be ready to build a tiny wall or hut.

 Creative Enrichment

1. What happens when you vary the ratio of sand and clay?

2. What happens if you make your mold too thick?

THE SCIENCE BEHIND THE FUN

Turning mud and sand into a building material is one of the great advances of civilization, dating back at least 9,000 years. Brick structures built almost 2,000 years ago still stand in India, while the Theater of Marcellus in Rome, though repaired several times, dates to 13 BC and is the oldest Roman building to use fired bricks. In the United States, the Taos Pueblo in New Mexico, made of sun-dried mud bricks, has been continuously inhabited for more than 1,000 years.

Using rocks to make a house or fort is great if you live in a place where there are lots of rocks. But much of the land where plants grow easily is covered with sand, silt, and clay. Being able to use soil for both farming and construction is a great benefit.

Early brick makers found that if they didn't wait long enough, their bricks would quickly fall apart. One way around waiting months for bricks to dry is to fire them in an oven. You can drive the water out of the bricks and start a chemical process that binds the clay and sand together. The problem is that you need a kiln, with temperatures reaching 1,800°F (982°C), and at least a week of firing. The result is a brick that can stand up to the chemical processes that we learned about earlier.

LAB 50

MAN OF STONE

You can let your imagination run wild by using just a few flat rocks to create a mythical *inukshuk*—a stone figure to guard your garden.

MATERIALS

- **Rocks**
- **Hammer and chisel**
- **Glue or superglue (optional)**
- **Wooden stand (optional)**

Safety Tips

- Watch your fingers! It's easy to get pinched when working with heavier rocks.

- If you use a hammer to shape your rocks, use eye protection.

PROTOCOL

STEP 1: Plan your shape so that you have an idea of what rocks to collect.

STEP 2: Gather your rocks from nearby sources. You can look in streambeds, along roads in ditches, travel to ocean beaches, or go to a nearby landscape supply company. Some parks have restrictions against removing material, so learn their regulations.

STEP 3: Stack your materials and create your shape. You may find that the pieces come together perfectly, or you may want to use a hammer, chisel, or even a steel file to get the shapes exactly as you want them.

 ## Creative Enrichment

1. Try different materials; do you like yours rough or polished?

2. What's the fewest number of rocks you can use? What's the biggest number of rocks you can use?

3. What are the best rocks to use—basalt, schist, granite, or sandstone?

THE SCIENCE BEHIND THE FUN

An inukshuk is a "likeness of a person" in the Inuit language. The Inuit live in the far north, in the Arctic regions of Alaska, Canada, and Greenland. The Inuit built their stone figures to show that someone was once at a place, that hunting or fishing would be good here, or to tell a traveler they were on the right path. In some cases, the inukshuk was made to say someone had great power or a place was to be respected. It was considered a bad thing to destroy such symbols.

When built to help for travel, the arms of the inukshuk would point in the right direction. When created for art, the shape could vary from small and simple to quite large, with several people involved in lifting the stones. Sometimes, the Inuit would build many structures in long lines along a favorite caribou trail. They could then steer the caribou toward a waiting group of hunters.

By using stone, the inukshuk can last a long time. You can build a large one for outside in the garden, or you can create a smaller structure for your bookcase. You may need glue to make sure your inside structure doesn't fall apart and cause damage to your furniture, but keep in mind that the true power of the piece comes from its ability to stand on its own. An inukshuk symbolizes the perseverance of the Inuit people to thrive in harsh conditions.

LAB 51

STACK 'EM UP

Unlike in the Man of Stone lab (page 134), in this exercise you'll stack rocks in a pyramid or a similar shape—the fun is seeing how many you can balance before they fall!

MATERIALS

- **Lab notebook and pen or pencil**
- **Rocks**
- **Ruler (optional)**

 Safety Tips

- Watch your fingers if you use large rocks.

- Don't work around glass or ceramics that can chip easily.

PROTOCOL

STEP 1: Plan your design. Draw a picture in your lab book to show what you want to make. Count the number of rocks you need.

STEP 2: Gather material. You can find smooth, round pebbles in most riverbeds or at the ocean beach. If you don't find enough natural material on your own, you can visit a landscape supply store.

STEP 3: Begin stacking. Start with big ones at the bottom and work your way up.

Creative Enrichment

1. How can you make the stack sturdier?

2. If you measure the stones, you can create a ratio of how much smaller each next stone must be for a solid pyramid.

3. Can you use little pieces of rock to wedge it tighter?

THE SCIENCE BEHIND THE FUN

Rock balancing, also called rock stacking, making cairns, and stacking stones, is an ancient practice. Stacking stones into cairns helps to mark trails that can become hard to follow during snow storms.

There is an annual Rock Stacking World Championship in Llano, Texas, with categories for height, balance, and art, among other things. In Nepal, different games played to see who can stack the last rock on top.

Some artists create wonderful forms that feature balance and counterbalance, using no glue or steel rods. These forms can be very delicate, and if there is a large earthquake, the structure will come tumbling down. To create your own earthquake detector, the trick is to build something that won't fall apart when a truck rolls past or a door is closed, but that is fragile enough to alert you to movement within the Earth's crust.

Visit earthquake.usgs.gov/earthquakes/map if your stones have mysteriously fallen to see if there was an earthquake nearby. Note the magnitude of the earthquake in your lab book. Check back frequently and note any earthquakes that did not knock down your structure.

Stacking rocks out in the wild is not always a good idea. You can disturb plants and animals by turning over stones, and you might surprise a spider, salamander, scorpion, or snake. National parks prohibit rock stacking. Elsewhere, such as at a river or at the ocean, you can rearrange rocks all you want, since the next tide or storm will change your creation and leave the material behind for the next person to enjoy.

CARING FOR CURIOS

Experiment with different ways to show off your treasures in a stylish display. You can do a lot with rough, natural stones when you are first starting out, and eventually you may want to learn how to tumble-polish rocks to make them even more attractive.

MATERIALS

- Assorted rocks, minerals, fossils, or other geological treasures such as pieces of wood, seashells, or beach glass
- Attractive glass, vase, jar, or other container
- Ribbons, plant material, or other interesting decorative material (optional)
- Scissors, wooden spoons, spatulas (optional)

 Safety Tips
 - Be very careful when mixing rocks and glass.

PROTOCOL

STEP 1: Gather your best treasures and get an idea of what you have.

STEP 2: Make a list in your lab book.

STEP 3: Find a nice container at a thrift shop that you can use for a display. To start with, you might want to just experiment with materials you find around the house. Check with a parent first!

STEP 4: Play around with your art—find more rocks of the same color, etc. You can layer red, white, and black rocks, for example. You can also decorate your curio container with things like ribbon.

Creative Enrichment

1. Try using colored sand—there are beaches with white, blonde, brown, black, or even green sands. You can layer the sands into attractive displays.

2. If you have a specimen you are proud of, create labels that describe what it is, where you found it, and other information.

3. Hand-sized specimens don't require a fancy glass. You can mount them on a stained, lacquered piece of wood, available at hobby stores, or they are easy to build. This encourages visitors to pick up your specimen and ask about it.

THE SCIENCE BEHIND THE FUN

Dating back at least to the Renaissance period in Europe, it was fashionable for rich merchants and community leaders to grandly display rocks, minerals, gems, jewelry, fossils, and other scientific novelties. *Curios* were things that could be called scientific marvels, and the more interesting, the better. Greeks and Romans described giant bones found in the Earth around the Mediterranean Sea as belonging to ogres, griffins, and other legends. Fossil collecting became popular in Europe in the early 1800s, and no curio collection was complete without a fossil bone or skull.

The term *curio case* was used to describe glass cabinets for showing off treasures. You can have fun with your own treasures by presenting them in the best way possible, building your own collection that you can be proud of. You may even want to put on display some of the things you created thanks to the labs in this book!

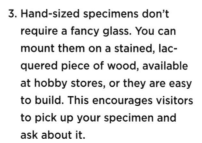

RESOURCES

Earth Science Week classroom activities

www.earthsciweek.org/classroom-activities

Check here for many more Earth science labs you can do at home.

Identifying rocks online

www.classzone.com, select "Science" as a subject and then click on the "Earth Science" book.

This site helps you identify rocks and minerals based on streak, color, density, and other details.

Kids.gov

kids.usa.gov/teens/science/geology/index.shtml

You'll find many more labs that explain geology and Earth science.

The National Crystal Growing Competition

http://www.cheminst.ca/outreach/crystal-growing-competition

Canadian high school students can grow their own crystals and compete for cash prizes.

INDEX